Then Comes The Joy

Then Comes The Joy

Mary Virginia Parrish

ABINGDON
Nashville

THEN COMES THE JOY

Copyright © 1977 by Abingdon

Library of Congress Cataloging in Publication Data

PARRISH, MARY VIRGINIA, 1911-
  Then comes the joy.
  1. Christian life—1960-   I. Title.
BV4501.2.P352   248   76-44383

ISBN 0-687-41439-3

Scripture quotations unless otherwise noted are from the Revised
Standard Version of the Bible, copyrighted 1946, 1952 © 1971, 1973 by
the National Council of Churches, and are used by permission.

Scripture quotations noted Phillips are from The New Testament in
Modern English, copyright © J. B. Phillips, 1958, 1960, 1972.

MANUFACTURED BY THE PARTHENON PRESS IN
NASHVILLE, TENNESSEE, UNITED STATES OF AMERICA

To

Ann Carter,
Allen, Allen III,
and Virginia

with love

Acknowledgments

My appreciation—

to Marianne Cox who believed my story needed to be written and who was willing to give days to correcting, typing, and retyping the manuscript

to her husband, Joe, and sons, Joe Jr. and Jimmy, who freed her from duties as wife and mother in order to help me

to countless friends who have shared my journey as I sought the reality of God through prayer and social awareness

to my parents who gave me a sense of personhood

and

to God who disclosed to me the person of Jesus, who gave me his Spirit and allows me to participate in his life.

Contents

Foreword

Mary Virginia Parrish shared forty-five wonderful days in Europe with me when the PWOC (Protestant Women of the Chapel) invited me to hold workshop rallies at various military bases in the fall of 1975. During that time, I read her manuscript of *Then Comes the Joy.*

In each chapter, Mary Virginia fearlessly faces the issues of life and openly shares the experiences which have led her to put Jesus Christ just where he belongs in our lives—right in the center. Not that this response was easy—it usually required stepping out tentatively and softly. But as soon as she knew God was leading her, she was willing to obey.

As you read her story, you will find yourself examining your own life with a better understanding of what happened to you in the past. More importantly, you will discover what God is trying to say to you in your present circumstances.

A new wind of the Spirit is moving across our traditional churches, and everywhere, people are responding and stepping out in faith. *Then Comes the Joy* describes such an adventure. If you are seeking God's guidance for your life, read this spiritual autobiography, and I'm certain that some of the guideposts given to Mary Virginia will become yours, too.

Rosalind Rinker

Prologue

In the heart of every man is a seeking, a knowing: there is a better way, there is a higher goal. Most men follow many paths before they turn to God. Yet as each goal is reached, dissatisfaction persists, and an inner voice whispers, "On and on . . . Don't stop short. There is more, much more."

The search continues. Will wealth and comfortable surroundings provide the good life? Will position and prominence within the community bring satisfaction? With fierce determination and concentrated effort man can achieve success, whatever his pursuit. Accomplishment may mean climbing on the shoulders of others; it may mean neglecting family and friends. It may even mean compromising former principles. But the drive to succeed keeps the nose to the grindstone, and the top is reached. There is no higher position within the firm, within the church, within the community; there is no larger income. And still—that deep desire remains—unfulfilled.

For many, an earthshaking experience is necessary to jar

them onto a totally new path. For most, it takes coming face-to-face with some hurt, some heartbreak, some situation for which they are unprepared. However, the end of sufficiency can be the beginning. The awareness that "of myself, I can do nothing" can be the entry into a whole new dimension of life. Need forces man to his knees with, perhaps, the first honest prayer of a lifetime. The words of Jesus, "Apart from me, you can do nothing," prompt the questions: How does man contact You? How does man become a part of You?

A tragic experience in my own life made me realize all my grit and determination, all my strength and will power could neither heal the brokenness of my heart nor answer the questions that haunted me. Not only did I lose a son at birth, but I had to confess I did not know a heavenly Father. Oh, lip service I gave. Intellectually, I believed. But I did not *know* him and I did not know how to contact him, or even if that were possible.

Please don't think me the lost sheep, the prodigal who had run into a far country. More like the elder brother, I was present in the right place (church), doing the right things (teaching, working, leading). I was moral and upright—with the too-often accompanying attitude of self-righteousness and judgmentalism.

I joined the church at an early age, I was an inquirer and questioner, always. My wonderful parents instilled ethical principles that I took to be the essence of Christianity. They required church attendance and went with their children, not content just to send them. They wanted us to be "good," and they gave us all they knew to give. I was taught "Now I lay me down to sleep," and had not grown beyond it. Neither home nor church taught prayer or the importance of it. In times of difficulty, I uttered a few frantic "help mes," but I relied on self-effort. It took me a long time to learn that man is not—nor was he meant to be—strong within his own strength.

When my baby died, I too was at the point of death. Only my broken heart and my confused mind functioned, and they cried out that agelong question, WHY? Why has this happened to me? Why is God punishing me? Why should my first child, a son, die? Oh, I knew the physical reasons: three days of extreme labor, too late for section, heart too weak after the struggle to be born. I wasn't asking scientific questions, my questions were theological. If God is love (I had to hang onto that anchor), why did he let my son die? If God is all powerful, why didn't he intervene? Are his hands tied? Is he dead, as some theologians said; or is he retired, as I thought, leaving all the action to man? Is he really active in today's world, or is he just at the beginning and the end of the cosmic drama?

My questions demanded answers. Either there was more than I had discovered, or else Christianity was, as some asserted, an escape, an opiate. If you have not known the pain of inadequacy, you cannot understand the imperative that drove me. Was God real? If so, I must find him.

The end of my self-sufficiency was the beginning of a life totally different.

I was given a book in which one word struck a responsive chord: During a crisis, we must not dwell on the "why" but on the "how." How can this tragedy be used to comfort others? How can creative good come out of sadness?

Redirecting my thoughts saved my sanity, but it did not stop my quest. Struggling on my own, I began reading books that centered more on an inward journey than an outward, which had always been my scene of action.

Two years passed, and I was faced with a miscarriage. The kindly doctor in the town where I was visiting offered concern and comfort, but no hope. Labor had begun, and he urged that I go to the hospital immediately. But I was reluctant, for deep within I knew there was a lonely battle to be fought. Agonizing "whys" were directed at God who was still unknown in any personal way. After a long struggle and by his grace (though I had no concept of the meaning of that word), my prayer suddenly changed from pleading to acceptance. I was able to pray for the first time in my life, "Not my will but thine be done." In a strange way that prayer was prayed through me; I was not the initiator. Even while praying, my rational mind was sorting out the meaning of my prayer—that I could accept the inevitable death of my second child without bitterness.

The moment I surrendered to God's will, I encountered God. No one had ever told me (or was it that I had not heard?) that man, a finite being, could meet God, the Infinite. Let me explain. I saw no vision, I heard no voice, but I knew his Presence. And time stood still. There were no questions in his Presence, no petitions—only glory. Then he left—as he had come. Again I was aware of my condition, and I knew I would be healed. I knew this baby would live.

Then the blessed Holy Spirit (that member of the Godhead about whom I knew nothing) began to teach me in words so very personal, "Mary Virginia, you have discarded the miracles. Your rational, reasonable religion has eliminated everything you cannot explain. Now I will show you—I am God. The miracle is meeting me. The outward manifestation that by the world's terms is called miraculous will come. Your baby will live."

And as he said, four and one-half months later, Ann Carter Parrish was born, a very special gift from God.

How does one who has not believed in miracles share with fellow skeptics? How can a sacred experience be verbalized? As I sought an audience, friends including my minister, gave me a pat of assurance as if to say: "We love you even if you are given to exaggerations and strange stories." Unless shared, the sense of the mystery and wonder can be lost from such a happening. The old pattern of thinking returns, memory fades, and doubt begins to make one wonder. So it was with me.

Five years later I met Dr. Frank Laubach. As I listened to him pray, I knew he knew the One I had encountered fleetingly. How thrilled I was to tell my story to someone who understood, someone who could help me. This saint of God had a vital relationship with him that I did not know was possible. He created within me a desire to know God, too, a real hunger that has grown with the years. Dr. Laubach recognized my appetite and gave me his little book, *Game with the Minutes,* an exercise in turning your thoughts Godward one second out of every minute until there is no separation in awareness (not feeling, but awareness). Dr. Laubach became my spiritual guide, and he advised my going to a Camp Farthest Out to learn how to pray and to be with others who were seeking. I wanted to go, but I was hesitant. What funny creatures we are, disliking ourselves as we are, yet fearful of change.

Four years went by before I went to Kanuga, an Episcopal assembly ground where the North Carolina Camp Farthest Out was meeting. There was such a conglomerate group of people who seemed so happy. They laughed at stories told by Glenn Clark, founder of CFO. I could hardly understand him, and I didn't think him funny. They did strange things, things that aren't so strange today—creative arts, creative writing, creative worship through devotion-in-motion. CFO was unlike any church camp I'd ever attended. These people sang and worshiped with a freedom that made me conscious of the dis-ease of my struggles to climb Jacob's ladder.

After three days in this company, it was revealed. This is the church—people from all walks of life, from all denominational backgrounds, drawn together by a common seeking to know God through prayer and the sharing of lives. Although at first I felt alien, the warmth of their love, their complete acceptance of me (even with my raised eyebrows) melted my resistance, and I began to learn the meaning of freedom and the art of loving.

A precious soul, a Quaker, Frank Olmstead, to whom I'd gone for counsel, asked a direct question that made me respond with a commitment such as I had never made before. Even now I can see the porch of that cottage by the lakeside when the question was asked. My answer required that I give up the right to myself, in so far as I knew myself.

At that moment, I entered into a new relationship with God, and he began to set me free. As a child I had accepted Jesus as Savior; now, as an adult I accepted him as Lord. He gave me the presence of his Spirit to be with me and in me—to interpret the Word to me, to disciple me, to teach me to pray. This drawing near to God was as new as if I had never entered a church. Amazing and tragically sad, isn't it?

The truth of Meister Eckhart's statement that men are willing to give up possessions, time, talent, but not the right to themselves has come home to me many times these past twenty years. In this new relationship, I have discovered being a Christian is not merely an intellectual assent to Someone or even conformity to certain rules. It is the possession of a new Spirit and the participation in a new life.

This pilgrimage never ends. There is much wandering in the wilderness. There are some peak experiences with valleys in between. There are plateaus, and you think you have arrived only to discover you have barely started. However, once the call is heard, the only response is that of giving "my utmost for his highest."

I have discovered that prayer is truly where God's action is. To learn to pray is to know him, to learn to live, to respond to life with a yes. No wonder the urgent request of those first disciples was: "Lord, teach us to pray" and, "Lord, teach us how to pray." Praying aright is essential, and it is learned only as any art is learned, through practice, plus the wonderful gift of prayer by the Spirit.

This book is a composite of my journey toward wholeness. May the glimmers of light, the glimpses of truth that have been disclosed to me, bring help to you. May your adventure in prayer bring to you a new and living way of knowing Him. With the psalmist, I can truly say,

> Thou hast turned for me my mourning into dancing;
>   thou has loosed my sackcloth
>   and girded me with gladness,
> that my soul may praise thee and not be silent.
>   O Lord my God, I will give thanks to thee for ever.
>   (Ps. 30:11, 12 RSV)

Chapter One

In the Beginning God

God granted me grace to pray "thy will be done . . ."
  before I knew
    the meaning of grace.
God granted me a miracle of healing . . .
  when I didn't believe
    in miracles.
God sent the Holy Spirit as my teacher . . .
  before I knew
    there was a Holy Spirit.
Such is the graciousness of God,
  and to him, I give thanks
    and praise his holy Name.

Where does one begin but with God? After a long time, I have learned he truly is the Hound of Heaven; he will not rest until he tracks us down. Then we can stop running, stop struggling, stop striving, and rest in him.

God is spirit, and we must worship him in spirit and in

truth. We are spiritual beings. Contrary to popular belief, cultivation of the spiritual life is essential for man to become fully alive. It has taken me many a year to understand spirit as reality, and matter but shadow. What a topsy-turvy world we live in.

Development of the spiritual life is not foreign to our nature. God made us for this purpose. He made us for himself. Since he is spirit, we must approach him and commune with him in spirit.

What is the spiritual life we are seeking? Is it merely introspection—a looking within to see what is happening? Is it an escape from practical, everyday living? A resounding no! The spiritual life is a life anchored in God—a life in which the secular as well as the sacred is shot through with glory.

Is it to be sought just by that small group of persons with special temperaments, with peculiar hungers—those who are of a particular religious order? Again, no. The seeking for the light and life of the spirit is the obligation and the privilege of every person who would follow Jesus. Many refuse the search under the guise of being unworthy; some attempt to live out the Christlike life under their own power, and fail; some hide behind the heresy, "I could never be like Jesus. After all, I'm just a human being."

Have we forgotten? Do we not know? He made us, common clay, to contain and to transmit his divinity. Else, why would Paul remind us that we are the temples of the living God? The purpose for which we are created demands that we acknowledge God as the source of all life. We are destined to grow into the likeness of Jesus who promised to abide in us.

Throughout history the writings of the saints agree that

there are three great movements in the growth of the soul. The first is an unconditional, utterly trusting, self-giving to God. The second is a daily drawing near to God through the Scriptures and through prayer. Then comes the third, a time of being used as his instrument.

Another description of the three-part pattern is: adoration of God, adherence to God, cooperation with God. To me, these three stages of growth can be described by the verbs "to abandon," "to abide," "to abound." These culminate in the verb "to be."

I recall so well the first time I was asked to lead a four-day school of prayer. Although I had spoken often and had given book reviews, which were really performances, this was a new experience. As the time drew near, I became more and more aware of my lack of spiritual depth. What did I have to say that would minister to others? How little I had to share of a spiritual nature. I expressed my fear to my friend Mary Webster, longtime colleague and evangelist with Dr. E. Stanley Jones. She comforted me with these words, "Don't worry, Mary Virginia. God is desperate. He'll use anybody."

And so he will. This is the amazing love of God. This is the implicit trust he places in those who seek him with all their hearts. Even in the process of being used, the speaker as well as the hearer is being taught by the Spirit. What a difference! I am no longer working for God, but he is doing his work through me.

Jesus said, "It is the Father who lives in me who carries out his work through me" (John 14:10 Phillips). He intends that each of us be able to utter the same words.

What seeming arrogance! What true humility! A shift of

22

roles: He is the initiator, he is the center from which all truth, all light, all life come.

When I first began the spiritual walk, Glenn Clark's book *I Will Lift Up Mine Eyes* served as a threat and a challenge. He urged his readers to become "athletes of the spirit." At first reading I found this book beyond belief. That man and God could enjoy such an intimate relationship was impossible. Thankfully, I was drawn to read the book a second time, this time more slowly, carefully following the suggested daily exercises. Though the second reading did not dispel my skepticism, it did kindle within me a great yearning, a great hunger to believe. It took a third reading—a living, a soaking in the book—for my disbelief to be swept away and real belief to be mine. Glory!

Glenn Clark has made a tremendous contribution to the spiritual development of thousands in our day. Through the vision given him for the Camps Farthest Out, he has offered persons the opportunity of going apart and learning to pray as Jesus prayed. He possessed the creative mind of God as few men have. I am grateful he was one of the speakers at the first camp I attended in 1955. The next year, Glenn Clark moved into the dimension of the spirit we call death, prepared as few are to enjoy the wonders of the heavenlies.

How graciously Jesus gives each of us the opportunity to enter the Holy of Holies, into the very presence of God. No longer is this privilege reserved for the High Priest alone. No longer does the Spirit make himself known only to a few prophets, as under the Old Covenant. Through the sacrifice of Jesus, the curtain was rent. The Holy of Holies is available to all who will enter.

As I ponder the mystery, the wonder, that any man,

every man, is extended an open-ended invitation to come into the presence of the Most High God at any time, any place, I bow in awe. Isn't it strange that we who would not dare refuse an invitation from the President of the United States, ignore that given by Almighty God.

Why would we want to spend eternity with God if we are unwilling to spend one hour a day in his presence? Why would we want to spend eternity with one we've never met, one whose language is foreign to us?

When I discovered prayer was the key to Dr. Laubach's intimacy with God, I made a decision. I would do whatever was necessary to have this same vital relationship. God allowed me to know such a closeness could be mine if I were willing to pay the price.

I was told of the need for a quiet time, a time set apart each day to commune with God. Always an activist, I found this a difficult assignment. However, I followed the suggested procedure and set a goal of fifteen minutes each morning to seek his presence.

With shame, I confess that fifteen minutes was the longest period of my day; I felt as if I were wasting time. Oh, to learn to center my mind on him. The more I tried, the more my mind became cluttered with thoughts of Girl Scout work, League of Women Voters legislation, Sunday school lessons, menus, and housework. I knew not how to listen.

One year after starting this discipline, I was at my second CFO to sit again at the feet of my guide Dr. Laubach. I determined to rise even earlier than the morning meditations. Despite my dislike of early rising, I saw the necessity for denial. During this early morning watch as I was reading

Psalm 46, the tenth verse leaped from the page in giant size, "Be still, and know that I am God."

How wonderfully God met my soul's sincere desire. How beautifully he filled me with his presence. I knew stillness for the first time in my life. Outward calm I could exhibit in proper ladylike fashion, but now, deep within, the turbulence was quieted, and I became one with him and with all creation in one mighty sweep.

Truly he will make himself known to those who seek—who seek him with all their hearts. Meeting him was worth everything. Knowing the reality of his presence is worth years of honest seeking.

In the beginning God walked and talked with Adam. Today, right here, right now, in the twentieth century, he walks and talks with those who have eyes to see, ears to hear. He yearns to manifest himself. How we need to cultivate a constant awareness. He is present! He is real! Allelulia!

The great Jewish theologian Martin Buber has said, "All real living is meeting." I agree. To truly meet is to discover the secret of living.

To pray aright is to meet God, to enjoy his friendship, to discover his guidance. To learn to pray is to learn to live, to meet life victoriously. Why have we neglected this important art? Thank God, he let my need be known to me. Thank God, he has brought into my life many persons of prayer to encourage, to instruct, to inspire me to make my inward journey. Thank God who is the beginning. Thank God for Jesus who through his suffering provided a new and living way for intimacy with the Father.

How marvelous to find that God yearns to have converse with us; to discover that as we seek him, he is seeking us. It is a double search. As we make discoveries, we find that he is making disclosures. What a rare privilege, and how our hearts glow within when his illumination comes. We can say with the blind man, "Once I was blind, but now I see!" After years of searching with our minds, we discover his wisdom is granted by his grace.

A new world is entered. A new Kingdom is our home, for suddenly we *are* at home, comfortable in his presence. Former discipline becomes delight. The difficult fifteen minutes of quiet time stretch into hours. Even then, there is reluctance to leave the place of quiet, joyous meeting.

For meeting is living, and real living is unbroken communion with the Father.

Chapter Two

Learning His Language

"Lord, teach us to pray." If God speaks today, I want to hear him. If his language is discernible, I want to learn it. If I am a citizen of heaven, as Paul indicates, then I must know the language of the King. Only through communication can I begin to relate to him. Prayer, as communication, is an art which must be learned. It is not monologue, but dialogue. Prayer requires listening and speaking, hearing and sharing.

Two things are essential if we would draw near to God. We must believe that God exists, and we must think it is worth the effort to seek him. Spiritual starvation comes from our neglect of devoting ourselves to prayer. This starvation is seen not only in those who are twice-a-year church attenders, but in many who are regular in their attendance.

We need to be reminded of the disciples' request, "Lord, teach us to pray. Lord, teach us how to pray."

Prayer held a very special place in the life of Jesus. For

27

him, prayer was not a routine formality, but a hallowed time for fellowship with the Father. The disciples watched him go out early in the morning to pray alone. He returned full of the Holy Spirit, his countenance radiant with a reflected glory.

The disciples saw a vast difference in his prayer life and theirs. What was his secret? Maybe they, too, could discover the key to the limitless power that Jesus manifested. The precepts that he taught were impossible to follow without God's enablement. So they said, "Lord, teach us how to pray."

Jesus answered the request of the disciples by giving them a prayer pattern. We refer to it as the Lord's Prayer. May we consider it.

Our Father who art in heaven—

When one truly enters into the presence of God, adoration is the natural response. To stand, to sit, or to kneel in the presence of the creator of the universe is an awesome experience. The divine-human encounter is a joy beyond description, yet it is always open to us.

So often we rush in, throw a list of petitions at God, rush out, and call it prayer. More and more time must be spent in awareness of the one with whom we speak—in simply adoring him.

How does one begin to adore God? By allowing him to capture our imaginations. Think on his majesty, his almightiness. Think on his unconditional love, his limitless grace. Think on the wonder that he has invited you to have fellowship with him.

The words of the psalmist help us to enter into his presence with an attitude of adoration: "Holy, holy, holy is the Lord." Take time to dwell on the holiness of God.

Think on the word "Father." What a loving name—not only the Father of Jesus, but our Father.

Once, following my radio interview with a young black man, he asked, "Mrs. Parrish, where have you lived all your life?" When I replied, "Hopkinsville, Kentucky, why do you ask?" he answered, "You do not think like most people around here. How did you come to feel as you do toward us blacks?"

"Robert, one day in church as I was praying, or maybe I should say *saying,* the Lord's Prayer, the words 'our Father' choked me. I was stabbed awake. I knew I could no longer call God Father unless I included the whole human race in the universal 'our.' From that experience I learned not only that truth is universal, but that the truly personal is always universal."

Hallowed be thy name—

Our fear of becoming chummy with God sometimes causes us to miss the thrill of awesome intimacy. "Holy is thy name." When we Christians think of God we think of Jesus, the complete manifestation of God, for he said, "He who has seen me has seen the Father." As we seek holiness we need look no further than Jesus for our pattern and our power. He is the all in all.

Thy kingdom come, thy will be done, on earth as it is in heaven—

All are guilty of seeking to change the mind of God. At the beginning, we really pray, "My will be done—of course, with thy blessings."

One of the primary purposes of prayer is to align our wills with his. Some years ago I read Margaret Slattery's *Thy Kingdom Come, But Not Now.* The content I forget, but the title continues to haunt me. This is our basic sin:

29

our refusal to live in that kingdom now, to let him be King of our lives, to recognize the primacy of God. As his will is done within each of us, we can live in that kingdom right here, right now.

The first three statements in the Lord's Prayer are directed toward our relationship to God; the last four point to our relationship to ourselves and to others.

Give us this day our daily bread—

God provides. He has obligated himself to provide for those who seek his kingdom first. Yet, he requires that we ask. The need to ask, to seek, to knock, causes us to question, If he knows all, why ask?

First, he commands that we ask. In obedience to him we must comply. Another reason for asking is to clarify our requests within our own minds, to become specific. Oftimes our prayers are so vague we don't recognize the answer when it is received. This stems from lack of trust. We are afraid to put God on the spot. What if he does not answer? What if he can not? What if Jesus made some promises the Father will not back up? All these thoughts go racing through our heads. They expose our ignorance of our heavenly Father who is completely able and most trustworthy.

God cares. Nothing is too small to escape his notice, nothing is too small for him to delight in doing for us. We miss the surprises he has by our failure to bring our everyday needs to him. I used to think God was only interested in the big, profound things of life. I have been slow to learn he cares about the tiniest request.

Recently, I was faced with a minor decision: Should I fly or drive to Atlanta to visit my daughter and her family? I had ambivalent feelings. There was the need to choose the less expensive mode of travel coupled with a fear of driving that distance alone. Such a fear was new to me. I had always depended on my husband for driving long distances. My travel pattern had had to change since his death. I expressed my anxiety to my daughter who said, "Mother, let's pray about this and ask God to give us a promise or definite direction." Her faith has always been greater than mine, simpler and more specific. The old concept that I shouldn't bother God about such trivialities still clung to me.

The following morning while reading the Sixteenth Psalm, these words captured my attention:

I will bless the Lord who gives me counsel;
  in the night also my heart instructs me.
I keep the Lord always before me;
  because he is at my right hand, I shall not be moved.
  Therefore my heart is glad, and my soul rejoices;
  my body also dwells secure.

(verses 7-9)

I knew "my body also dwells secure" was meant for me. It would be safe for me to drive to Atlanta.

Imagine our delight when my daughter, without prior knowledge of my using the Psalms for devotional reading, received the very same verse as the promise on which to stand. Coincidence? Oh no—these are the serendipities which the Lord gives to those who ask in childlike faith. How wonderful to know we have a Father who cares even about such mundane things as whether we drive or fly to Atlanta.

And forgive us our debts, as we also have forgiven our debtors—

THEN COMES THE JOY

Does this mean God's forgiveness is conditional? Must we prove ourselves before he will grant us forgiveness? Surely the Father who was willing to give his only Son for us is not now requiring us to shape up before he will forgive.

No, of course he will forgive, he wants to forgive. But we cannot accept forgiveness until we are willing to forgive others. We cannot contain his forgiving spirit and an unforgiving spirit simultaneously. Willingness to forgive is so important, even to the point of making restitution when it is possible and necessary.

And lead us not into temptation—

The way in which this is recorded is confusing. I won't even try to explain other than to say God tests, God does not tempt. Let us not be led into temptation beyond our power to resist. We should pray that God will be our protector against enticing evils.

But deliver us from evil—

Jesus came to set us free from those things that imprison, that cripple, us. The prayer of deliverance is an appropriate prayer when evil overcomes us.

For thine is the kingdom and the power and the glory, for ever. Amen.

Even though this is an addition, what a wonderful ending to any prayer. As we enter his kingdom at the beginning of prayer, so we declare his kingship at the end. Thanksgiving and praise should always be our closing theme. Let it be, Lord, let it be. Estelle Carver, a great Bible teacher, suggests that the Lord's Prayer can be an excellent prayer of intercession for others. Insert the name of the person for whom you are praying. "Let thy kingdom come in Mary; let thy will be done in Mary," and so forth.

"Frank, teach me to pray." Addressing him by his given name was not a sign of disrespect but the custom at CFO, where all titles are dropped and we become one, all children living in the kingdom of God.

Like those early disciples who made the request of Jesus, I made the same request of Frank C. Laubach, Mr. Literacy for the World. I knew he spoke to Someone who was real and that he knew him.

Although I am indebted to many persons who have shown me the necessity of a dedicated devotional life if one would follow Jesus, it is to Frank Laubach I am most indebted. I will share some of the secrets he disclosed. May they create within you the same desire, the same willingness, to devote yourself to learning the art of prayer.

1. Keep your mind centered on God. Practice his presence.
2. Deliberately train yourself to think of him, his nature, his kingdom. Saturate yourself · in the Scriptures, particularly the Gospels, for learning about Jesus. Try to think about God one second out of every minute. Only those who have made this effort can appreciate the proportions of the task.
3. Keep reminders around. Dr. Laubach showed me a small folder in which he had a collection of his favorite pictures of Jesus. This he carried with him as he traveled about the world teaching illiterates to read. I can remember his saying, "Now these are only crutches, but it is better to walk with a crutch than not to walk at all."
4. Talk with God simply as a child talks to his earthly father. Keep an interior conversation going all day.
5. Fill in all the spaces of the day with thoughts of God.

At the stoplight, instead of fretting, pray; in the airport let all the strangers be prayer subjects; pray as you clean, do dishes, and so forth.

6. Set apart a special time every day for being with God, for pondering his Word. Take pen and paper to prayer. Write down thoughts which come.

7. Let your first thought in the morning be of him. Recite scripture, "This is the day which the Lord has made. Let us rejoice and be glad in it." Let your last thought before falling asleep be of him. Then your subconscious will feed on that all night; you will "feel the gale of the Holy Spirit go forward even in sleep."

(Thomas a Kempis, 1386-1471)

"Frank, you pray differently from me. Teach me. How do you pray?" I directed this question to Frank Olmstead. We were in the prayer room at the Kentucky Camp Farthest Out. This man, who had such a great capacity for silence, spoke so intimately to Jesus. "I only address myself to God," I told him. "Do you pray to Jesus?"

Frank never answered a question such as that directly. He had learned to make others search for answers. I knew Jesus was not as real to me as to Frank. In fact, I was reluctant to talk much about Jesus. In speaking to God, a sufficient distance existed. Somehow, Jesus brought God just a little too close for my comfort. Frank Olmstead talked so simply with Jesus—distance diminished, formality faded. A dear unseen friend was present. Our formal prayers often deny us such intimacy.

God brought into my life a prayer partner. Mary Helen and I later agreed we would never have chosen each other. How different we were. She never joined organizations; I was involved in many. She never attended a committee meeting; I was "committeed" to death. She was casual to the point of irresponsibility (in my opinion); I had an overly active sense of responsibility. She felt no great world concern; the world weighed heavily upon my shoulders. But we both were seekers after Truth. We both, through differing experiences, had been placed on Jesus' way of prayer. We both knew God had brought us together. We learned from one another—sometimes painfully, oftimes delightfully.

Mary Helen became a member of a little prayer group that I, always the organizer, had started in our church. It was composed of three Sunday school teachers and Mary Helen, who had never prayed aloud. We teachers had no difficulty verbalizing prayers. Had we not led in prayer for years? How precise of language, how correct of speech, how studied the proper "thees" and "thous."

We four met week after week, and something happened. We forgot to *say* prayers. We prayed. And Mary Helen felt free to speak a word with the Lord. At this point, Mary Helen made this astute observation, "Either you all are getting worse at praying or I am getting better."

So, we began to discover the difference when God became our audience. We became comfortable in his presence. We did not use the King James language that was stilted to us. We spoke to him simply as a child to a loving Father.

"Starr, teach me your secret of prayer." Starr Daily, a confirmed criminal who was dramatically changed from crime to Christ, truly knew the meaning of the redemptive love of God. He became such a man of prayer that hundreds sought his counsel. To sit in his presence was to sense deep wells of stillness.

Once when he was in my home I sought to wrest from him his secrets. Hopeful that he would give me some easy shortcut to a life of prayer, I asked, "Starr, how does one learn to pray?" When he told me he had three rules, I was delighted. At last it was within my reach. Then he said, "The first rule is *pray*. The second rule is *pray*. And the third is *pray*."

I had sought a quick, simple formula, but prayer introduces you to a Person whose presence is to be cultivated. There are no shortcuts.

"Glenn, teach me about prayer and guidance. Can someone receive guidance for another?" This time I was questioning Glenn Harding, a man of deep prayer. We were at the annual association meeting of CFO. I had just been tapped on the shoulder by a lady, a stranger to me, who said, "I think God wants you to replace me in the job I am going to resign." Her sense of certainty baffled me.

I related the incident to Glenn who very wisely said, "How do you feel about the job? Do you sense God is wanting you to respond affirmatively?"

My answer was, "No, it would mean my moving from my home. Besides, it doesn't seem right. However, I have been praying for a job since my husband's death and that lady seemed so sure. I do want to do God's will. Does another person know God's will for me?"

Glenn replied: "You must be willing, for God often uses other people to be his spokesmen. However, no one can receive your guidance for you."

I returned home to wrestle with this until I had no will of

my own and could submit to whatever God had for me. This was a great learning opportunity for me. Since I never got the "go sign," my guidance was "wait."

The Gospel of Luke gives us a clear picture of the prayer life of Jesus. As we catalogue the number of references to prayer we realize his prayers were largely for three purposes: (1) for fellowship with the Father, for the sheer joy of being alone in his presence; (2) for guidance, once, we are told, he prayed all night seeking his Father's will regarding the selection of the disciples; and (3) for enabling power to fulfill his ministry on earth.

The importance of confession. We have to deal with one prayer area which Jesus did not have—that of confession. He urged us to confess our sins, one to another. Not until I read Dietrich Bonhoeffer's *Life Together* did I see how lacking confession was in most persons of the Protestant faith. Often we remain burdened with unforgiven guilt because of our pride. To confess to another specific sin is a humiliation, but it is also the death of pride.

A confessor must be aware of two needs, the need for complete confidence and the need for recognition that we are all sinners, cleansed only by the suffering Christ and his atoning blood. "It is only God's offer of grace, help, and forgiveness that could make us dare to enter the abyss of confession. We can confess solely for the sake of the promise of absolution. Confession as a routine duty is spiritual death; confession in reliance upon the promise is life. The forgiveness of sins is the sole ground and goal of confession."

We, by the authority granted those in Christ, claim absolution, and the confessant is freed of guilt. "By the blood of Christ, you are forgiven." How beautiful are those words. We all need to hear them verbalized through a Christian brother. Thus all believers can minister to one another in this priestly function authorized by Christ, the High Priest, the King of Kings and Lord of Lords.

The power of intercession. No prayer is more beautiful in all Scripture than Jesus' priestly prayer in John 17. As he prayed for those first disciples, so he urges us to intercede for others.

If you were told you could help change the world from darkness to light, from despair to hope, would you accept the challenge? We are told in Scripture: "If my people who are called by my name humble themselves, and pray and seek my face, and turn from their wicked ways, then I will hear from heaven, and will forgive their sin and heal their land" (II Chron. 7:14).

> Justice is turned back,
>   and righteousness stands afar off;
> for truth has fallen in the public squares,
>   and uprightness cannot enter.
> Truth is lacking,
>   and he who departs from evil makes himself a prey.
>   The Lord saw it, and it displeased him
>   that there was no justice.
> He saw that there was no man,
>   and wondered that there was no one to intervene.
>   (Isa. 59:14-16a)

Why is there no one to intervene? (1) We have not prayed enough to believe in the power of prayer. (2) Intercession is a hidden ministry. We want an audience; we want praise; we desire credit. (3) We lack the willingness to persist into faithfulness.

Yet, we have the pattern of Jesus before us who lived out a life of prayer on earth and is now seated at the right hand of God praying. "Consequently he is able for all time to save those who draw near to God through him, since he always lives to make intercession for them" (Heb. 7:25).

I wish you could know the joy I experienced when I first became aware Jesus was ever interceding for me. In the mystery of infinity he is able to pray for each of us simultaneously. I am never alone in my prayers; he is constantly seeking to draw me into the very presence of God's love and grace. And Jesus, the perfect intercessor, invites us to share in this ministry.

Imagine what would happen if thousands began serving as intercessors for our government. The course of history could be changed. God honors the prayers of those who persistently seek him. What if each church had a prayer army? A group of "inactive" members could quietly change the whole climate of the church through intercession.

Glenn Clark's parable of the fanner bees caught my imagination. These are the bees that spend all their strength constantly fanning their wings and, in so doing, keep the hive fresh and cool by circulating the air. I presented this challenge to a shut-in, a woman bedridden with crippling arthritis and asthma. She was excited over being of use to the church she loved and had actively served until illness prevented her leaving home.

Together we searched the rolls of the church for those who could serve as a telephone committee. Miss Annie served as the captain with five lieutenants under her. Weekly, these would be contacted for reports. If there were special requests, they were immediately channeled to the five who in turn called five.

Miracles of healing and of conversion were reported within that little army of intercessors. They became aware of the power of prayer. Not only did that army discover a new and deeper relationship to God, but they discovered a new avenue of service. No longer were they inactive, placed on the no-use shelf. They were vitally aware of and participating in every facet of the church's life. They were no longer isolated; they had a sense of place.

Miss Annie Jackson was an amazing prayer leader. One day while I was visiting her, she revealed one secret of her joyous nature. "Whenever I feel unusually bad, I call someone and try to bring them joy." She had learned the lesson of giving-receiving.

Perhaps you are thinking that prayer may work for a church group, but should not be mixed up with government. Intercession is needed there, and prayer does work. Shortly after I became executive director of the Commission on Human Relations for the City of Hopkinsville, I experienced real discouragement. What could one person do? No human effort seemed to alter the growing hostility and tension between blacks and whites. I sought God's guidance. An intercessory prayer group was the answer. So there came into existence a small interracial group who meet weekly to pray specifically for this situation and other areas of concern within our city, state, and nation.

There are no clear measuring rods for prayer, but I know the petitions earnestly placed by that small group on the altar of prayer diminished the tensions and led to improved relationships in our city. I can witness to the supportive help the group gave me weekly as I shared with them areas for which we would pray. Out of these prayers came the idea for the Mayor's Prayer Breakfast that is part of the annual Human Relations Week in our community.

Prayer is a powerful spiritual weapon. "Prayer is for women and weaklings." I resented these words when they were spoken by a minister to one of his deacons who, in desperate need of help, had been invited to join a prayer-sharing group. I no longer resent the words. I agree. Prayer is for those who acknowledge their weakness, those who can say without shame, "Without God, I am nothing."

What false concepts we have of prayer. Prayer is not a pious exercise, not just a frill to our religious life. Prayer is not something you do when you get too old to work, too tired to act, too withdrawn to be sociable. Prayer is not an extra. It is as essential for spiritual health and growth as breathing is for physical well being.

Prayer is something which everyone does, but few really know how. Even primitive man cries out to something—out there. All religions use some form of prayer. Prayer is natural. Making sounds is natural for a baby; yet it takes training to learn to speak, more training and practice to speak well. A cry for help will come from an atheist, but effective prayer is the result of discipline.

Concentration is required. When I was leading a school of prayer for the Protestant Women of the Chapel, the chaplain in Fort Leavenworth, Kansas, told me that the Aramaic definition of prayer is rearranging the mind. What an excellent description. In Isaiah 55:8 we read: "For my

41

thoughts are not your thoughts, neither are my ways your ways, says the Lord." May we unite in praying, "Rearrange our minds, O God, so that your thoughts may become our thoughts."

Dedication is required. Only those who truly seek him, those who are willing to forego good things to do the one thing needful, as Jesus told Martha, will find him to be real. Then prayer becomes
not words—only Presence.
not advice—only silence.
When the external falls away and
   only the eternal remains,
when scattered thoughts are gathered
   into singleness of mind,
      the human and the Divine meet.
What mystery revealed! What awe experienced!
   The unseen becomes real and we are one.
No longer needing the laws, the symbols, the crutches,
   only a willingness to give all to
      the pursuit of God;
   yet knowing
     it is his pursuit and
       we are caught,
         never to escape.

Chapter Three

Becoming a New Creature

"Behold, I make all things new" (Rev. 21:5). Jesus came preaching the gospel of the kingdom of God. It was and is the great passion of his life. Now, as then, the word "kingdom" creates within our minds visions of thrones, diamond tiaras, golden scepters.

The overthrow of Rome was the longheld dream of the Jewish nation. When Jesus proclaimed, "The time is fulfilled, and the kingdom of God is at hand" (Mark 1:15), the hearts of the Jewish people jumped for joy. At last their Messiah had come. The Kingdom would be established. They would be freed from the tyranny of Rome.

Yet, the Master spoke of a different kind of kingdom—a kingdom still difficult to fathom. It is not a kingdom so much of doing as of being, a kingdom in which persons express attitudes very different from the world's—attitudes of humbleness, teachableness, singlemindedness, mercy. Attitudes that express hunger to live within that kingdom and that show an increasing desire for righteousness.

43

The kingdom of God was not a totally new figure of speech, but Jesus gave it a completely new meaning. In the secular vernacular the Kingdom was emphasized almost to the exclusion of God. Jesus came preaching the almightiness of the Father. The Kingdom was his. The Kingdom was not to be built by men, but to be received as a gift from God to men.

The Kingdom was not a place, but a presence—God reigning supreme within an individual life, God reigning supreme within the world. The kingdom of God in the heart was a moral and spiritual imperative. It was individual yet social, personal yet universal; it was present yet future. So paradoxical did it seem that those who saw and heard were confused.

While in the wilderness being tempted by Satan, Jesus had to cast aside the very real temptation to turn stones into bread, a sure way to win favor and an audience. Why did he later feed the multitudes through the use of the same power? Satan's temptation was that of using his power for the sake of gaining a following, for dealing with the external before he revealed the eternal. Jesus rejected the shortcut method. He is still trying to teach us that the end does not justify the means. He is still instructing those of us who would look for a way to live out the Christian life-style other than the hard, narrow way of which he spoke.

Over and over we ask, "If it is the Father's good pleasure to give us the kingdom (Luke 12:32), what part do we play?" A gift cannot be a gift until it is received. Although we cannot thwart the Kingdom's coming, it does appear we can delay it by our basic sin—refusal.

"Truly I say to you, unless you turn and become like

children, you will never enter the kingdom of heaven" (Matt. 18:3).

Paul makes a challenging statement regarding "apprehending that for which I have been apprehended" (Phil. 3:12 KJV). I had to come to grips with the fact that I had not "grasped that for which I was grasped" (*loc. cit.*, Phillips). In the process of growing up I had discarded many truths of the Bible; they were too simplistic for the sophisticated age in which we lived. In an effort to be reasonable and rational, I had tossed aside as no longer relevant that which I, with limited understanding, could not explain.

I had forgotten that Jesus said, "Except you become as a little child you cannot enter the kingdom." This was brought home to me by my daughter when she was of kindergarten age. Before putting her to bed I had told her the Bible story of Jesus healing the man who was born blind. When she questioned why the people doubted the miracle and continued to ask the man and his parents if he really had been blind prior to the touch of Jesus, my explanation was, "Well after all, Ann Carter, it would be hard for anyone to believe that a man could take a little dirt from the earth, spit upon it, apply it to blind eyes and cause a man to see." Never shall I forget the simple childlike faith expressed as she looked at me and said, "But they just didn't know Jesus, did they?"

Her question drove me to my knees in my bedroom with the confession: "And I don't know Jesus, either. Please, Lord, show me how to believe."

Had I not made a child's profession of faith at the age of ten? Can you say that was not valid? It was valid in that there was belief of an intellectual nature. I believed in the historical Jesus. I would have liked to follow him. He had captured my child's heart. But I did not know the foundation fact of the Kingdom, becoming a new creature.

Among my many discards was, "You must be born anew." I had been baptized in water, but I failed to recognize that Jesus said, "Truly, truly I say to you, unless one is born of water and the Spirit, he cannot enter the kingdom of God" (John 3:5).

The Bible states it quite emphatically, but at that time, I was reading the Bible only to prove what I had already decided was true. Amazing how we can deceive ourselves so completely. I was not in the habit of going to the Bible to discover its message. There is no question but that our day is suffering from the underemphasis of terms like "conversion" and "regeneration." People strive to live the new life while still an "old man."

Even half-hearted attempts to live the Christian life under human effort and power end in frustration. We settle for less for we can see no hope. C. S. Lewis reminds us that Jesus did not come to make "nice men" but "new men." Mere improvement is not redemption. It is not like teaching a horse to jump better and better, but like turning a horse into a winged creature. Radical change is required. A total abandonment of the old that we may become what we are meant to be—new creatures. Even the lowly caterpillar undergoes a revolution to become a beautiful butterfly. If God planned such for the caterpillar, is it any wonder that he wants to do a revolutionary work in us?

Only those who are willing to give up the struggle of becoming, to "let go and let God" remake them, can live in the kingdom of God. God makes Jesus the standard and no man can meet that. Only the indwelling Christ can meet the demands set down in the Sermon on the Mount. Purposely, he made the task impossible for man to attain.

It seems Jesus assumes man will go through different stages. The first, the spontaneity of childhood, when faith is not clouded by doubt, when belief is very simple and mystery is easy to accept. Second, life crowds in and man becomes imprisoned with fears, with doubts, with inhibitions. Then third, man becomes new. Life is again spontaneous when man can retain a child's heart and a child's direct simplicity coupled with a man's courage and intellect.

To grow up is to come face to face with one's unworthiness. To accept the gift of new life through the atoning work of Jesus on the cross requires the recognition that all our struggles toward "goodness" are not sufficient. There persists within most of us the false concept that we are placed here to earn heaven. How pridefully we count our Brownie points. That pride must go through a crucible before we are ready to have revealed to us our poverty. There is a "time" for all of us. God's patience is limitless. He waits.

My time came in this way. Through my skillful manipulations, I had arranged for some "spiritual giants" to be in our community. I knew how much the *other* people needed them. For two weeks I soaked in their inspired teachings. Whether others benefited or not from the exposure to these saints, I do not know. But the Lord was working on me as he promises to do once we have said, "OK, take over. I'm weary of running my life. You make out the agenda."

Full to overflowing with resolve and desire to serve the Lord, I was on my way to Owensboro, Kentucky, to give a

THEN COMES THE JOY

World Day of Prayer talk for Church Women United. I do not know exactly what a vision is, but as I drove, there was imprinted upon my mind's eye a picture. It was as if I saw God. In front of him was a stone altar much the size of the communion table that stands in the church where I am a member. In front of the altar I stood, a figure frightened and insignificant, yet filled with a tremendous desire to bring something to God as an offering. I wracked my brain as to what I could give him and the thought came, "You can speak; you can organize. Bring these." And, in my mind's eye, these gifts were in my hands as I raised them to God.

The agony of what happened still causes my heart to tremble. From behind that altar came a mighty arm which ruthlessly swung down to sweep these, my gifts, out of my hands. An even mightier voice said, "I do not want your gifts. I do not need your gifts."

Unless you have stood before the Lord empty-handed and naked, you cannot grasp the pain of this moment. So overcome with sorrow was I that my weeping caused me to drive through a tollgate. Then I had to back up, search for change in my purse, all the while being looked at by the gatekeeper with understandable alarm.

I was still seeking to deal with such a devastating experience when I heard a voice speak so lovingly, "Mary Virginia, will you never learn? It is I who bring the gift. Look, here is the Gift." And the eyes of my heart were again brought to the stone altar. It was no longer bare; the form of Jesus was there.

Even as I recount this years later, that awful emptiness overcomes me, and I bow in awe and repentance. If this were not my time of inward crucifixion, I only pray that

God will give me the strength to bear a more soul-shaking experience.

I turned to Starr Daily for counsel for this event left me in a baffled state for several months. The God whose love had held me so warmly and firmly startled me with his seeming cruelty. I needed to learn he is a God of judgment. To preach a God of love without a God of judgment is to preach sentimentality, just as to preach God as judge without God as love is cruelty. He judges only to correct, and correct me he did.

He had to show me in an unmistakable way that only as we are weak, totally dependent, can we receive his strength. The roles were reversed. He gives, I receive. Receive, receive, receive has been constantly drummed into my head and heart since that very special day in my spiritual pilgrimage.

Only as our souls are awakened to our need and we are humbled before the Lord, can God do that which he wants to do with our lives. Regeneration—being "born again"—makes man know that he has received something as a gift from Almighty God, and not because of his own attainment or his own goodness.

I am grateful to Dr. Nels Ferre for his teaching on the book of Romans at the first quadrennial of the Christian Women's Fellowship at Purdue University. Paul's treatise on grace is not contrary to the teachings of Christ as I had been led to believe. Certainly, grace was a level of life I had not experienced.

Man can live life on three levels: (1) instinct, where all the physical desires dominate our whole beings; (2) the law, when we, like the elder brother, do the right things but for the wrong reasons (there again we see the good as enemy of the best); and (3) under grace, which fulfills the law and sets one free to live in childlike faith—where wonder, mystery, "belief in belief," and love are not hampered or imprisoned by legalism. We open wide our lives to receive the gift of his Spirit.

My good friend Norman Grubb bases his whole teaching on grace, and he has helped many to be set free from unforgiven guilt. As our eyes are opened to this new dimension that can be lived only when we receive his Spirit, we know that this life is as high above the human as the human is above the animal, the animal above the plant. Not through any goodness on our part, but through the redemptive work of Jesus on the cross. His is a gift that cannot be explained, but can be appropriated.

Once we have been set free to live a new life-style, we see the folly of trying to follow Christ without the Spirit of Christ. How duty-bound, how earthbound we are. We forget that we are spiritual beings who must have new eyes to see into the world invisible.

This earth-world is too much with us. We fail to become spiritually sensitive, constantly aware of God and his reality and his kingdom which is eternal. Yes, kingdom-living demands that we become new creatures. It is his almighty work, not ours. Our part is a surrender, a giving-up the right to ourselves, a saying, "Here am I. Do with me as you like."

What is it that keeps us from yielding? Why is surrender so difficult? Is it that we don't trust God? Has our intellectual approach, which can never fathom God, made us insensitive to spiritual truths, which must be spiritually discerned? We need to examine ourselves and see just how we meet life. What is our response?

BECOMING A NEW CREATURE

God has placed me in life situations that have required me to observe carefully not only my own behavior patterns, but those of others as well. Although it is never safe to generalize and to categorize, I must do so in this case. With that apology, I present what seem to be the three main categories into which most persons fit.

1. There are those persons who escape life.
2. There are those who fight life.
3. There are those who say yes to life.

Perhaps we all go through each of these phases at different times. Perhaps we move from one to another, but one of these responses is generally our pattern.

Strangely enough, we meet death in much the same way as we meet life. In my own experience, the ways in which I have faced death have mirrored my responses to life.

My first significant encounter with death was the sudden death of my only brother. It was the first time I had ever seen my parents bereft, and somehow it became my responsibility to make many of the necessary arrangements. I refused to think about it. Like an automaton, I moved through those days. So thoroughly did I do the job of escaping that I almost believed they would discover another body when the corpse arrived from Texas where my brother had died enroute to a family reunion. With steely determination, I set my jaw and refused to let sorrow run its healthy, normal course. What damages there are to soul and body from such an attitude.

A second way of meeting death—or life—is to fight it. The death of my young son was met with that age-old why? I would not let go. I continued to fight the fact that he did not live. Anguished thoughts kept haunting me. Did

God punish his children this way? Did God care? Did God not think we were fit parents? All these questions would give me no peace, only inward war.

A third way of meeting death is to say yes to death as a part of life—not try to escape, not fight, but simply accept the full realization. This is fact. My husband's death was sudden—from perfect health to death within a span of thirty minutes. Twenty years and a long spiritual pilgrimage separated my son's and my husband's death. During those years of walking in a growing awareness of God, I had learned to turn to him quite naturally and seek his wisdom at any crisis.

As I saw my husband die I sought God's guidance and he answered, "Give thanks." What a strange request for a loving Father to make. Yet, I had learned obedience was essential if my lines of communication were to remain open. I tried to give thanks. I searched for specific areas of thankfulness. I could thank God that Cliff did not have to suffer a long illness. I could thank God that Cliff, an engineer and an outdoorsman, did not have to suffer invalidism. Then God gave me a scripture. "It is a good thing to give thanks to the Lord, to sing praises to thy name, O Most High; to declare thy steadfast love in the morning, and thy faithfulness by night" (Ps. 92:1, 2).

That scripture became my anchor. I clung to it day and night. As I was enabled to give thanks, the ministry of the Holy Comforter became so real that underneath the sorrow was the deep joy of his abiding presence. It is true, just as Jesus said, "Blessed are those who mourn, for they shall be comforted." To experience the presence of the Comforter is a joy unspeakable. Then one knows, with that deep knowing only his Spirit can give, this which we call life is but a shadow of that which is to come. Life is eternal, and in him there is no death. Alleluia.

About six weeks after Cliff's death, God so gently and lovingly reminded me, "And do you know, you didn't even ask *why*?" He does let us get an occasional glimpse of some progress we have made. It would be too dangerous for him to let us see all, for the pride which he had worked so hard to eradicate would raise its head.

As we say yes to death, neither trying to escape its grim reality nor fighting it as if life had played an unfair trick upon us, there comes a new openness to God and to persons. The love, which is usually so timidly given, pours forth in a flood from those who come to comfort and to share in the sorrow. Compassion overcomes any shyness at saying I love you. Even as my daughter and I received the gift of love from friends, I was conscious of the rhythm of giving and receiving and yearned that such freedom could be ours under less stressful conditions. For as I was free to receive love, it became, like mercy, twice blessed. "It blesseth him that gives and him that takes." God demonstrated the healing power of love in such a way that I knew he was saying, "Don't waste your sorrow." The paradox remains—joy and sorrow simultaneously experienced. A new awareness that joy is an inside job, fulfilled by the indwelling Christ.

All life seems to follow a somewhat similar pattern. We can miss life by our unwillingness to face life, whether it is personal tragedy or a social condition. We can pull the mental curtain, shutting out those things we dare not face, yet doing untold damage to ourselves inwardly. We are meant for wholeness, and when we cut off a portion of our lives, we impair all life.

THEN COMES THE JOY

We fight those things we do not like; we fight to defend our position, our rightness. We fight change, inevitable as it is. Although facing a situation and fighting it is healthier than seeking the escape route, it ultimately ends in defeat.

Within the Christian context, to say yes to life is to say yes to Jesus who is life. Some of us rebellious ones have to go through all these behavior patterns before we, weary from the struggle and disillusioned by failures, come to the end of our sufficiency. Only then are we willing, like the prodigal, to return to the Father and say, "Make me over. I am ready to exchange my fighting, assertive self for your nature."

I remember when I made this exchange at a Christian ashram conducted by Dr. E. Stanley Jones. At the close of a service he invited those who wished to make a more complete surrender to come forward and kneel. I was among the first, for the Hound of Heaven had been on my heels for some time. When we knelt Dr. Jones prayed, then he said, "Your life for His life. What a swap!"

The path of surrender has been the path of all who would find meaning and purpose in life. In his memoirs, *Markings,* published three years after his death, Dag Hämmarskjold, former Secretary-General of the United Nations, wrote:

I don't know Who—or what—put the question. I don't know when it was put. I don't even remember answering. But at some moment I did say YES to Someone—or Something—and from that hour I was certain that existence is meaningful and that, therefore, my life, in self surrender, had a goal.

Chapter Four

Life After Birth

A single voice singing "He Lives" was soon joined by the voices of our entire group as we stood that chilly January morning in the Garden of the Tomb outside Jerusalem. One could easily imagine the awesome moment when Mary Magdalene, coming to that rock-hewn tomb, found the stone rolled to one side and the tomb empty.

I was glad that our guide, a young Anglican priest, shared his impressions of a recent visit by Dr. Christian Barnard, the noted surgeon who first performed a successful heart transplant. Pondering the mystery of the Atonement, Dr. Barnard had said that he could perform a heart transplant which might extend life for three days, three months, or even three years, but Jesus does a heart transplant which is eternal. Every Christian must receive a brand new heart—a revolutionary experience.

Gerald Kennedy points out a false assumption which calls for correction:

THEN COMES THE JOY

Religious education went on the wrong path when it tried to make Christianity an almost automatic process. It was thought that a child might become a Christian and never know he had been anything else. The ideal was to bring young people into the fellowship gently and gradually so that no crisis would occur in their lives. But this approach misunderstood the personal nature of the gospel and the fact that a man has to say YES to it. He has to know he has been confronted, and he has to know that he has accepted and been accepted. First, a man hears God say "Thou art the man." Secondly, he replies, "Thou art my God."

This Divine-human encounter brings forth a new life which must be nurtured if growth is to take place. Without day-by-day nourishment, spiritual starvation sets in. Jesus spoke of the Word of God being his food. He said he had other food which those first disciples knew not of. Those whose goal is spiritual maturity must become engaged in a new life-style—living a life devoted to God and nourishing the new life within them through Bible-reading and prayer.

There are many Bible scholars who have never read the Bible as spiritual food. Necessary as study of the Bible is, a distinction must be made. Reading the Bible devotionally is not for the purpose of knowing the Bible, but for knowing God.

Bill was a minister with a background of forty years in the pastorate. He had degrees from prominent seminaries in the United States and Europe. He brought his son, who had obvious needs, to a Camp Farthest Out. The last night of the camp, I was in conversation with Bill. He questioned me regarding God at work in today's world, whether miracles were still possible, how to know the voice of God. After two hours of his questioning and my witnessing to my journey from skepticism to faith, I shared with Bill the tremendous difference in knowing about God and knowing God.

I even asked him the direct question, "Bill, do you *know* Jesus?" The agony of his soul answered before his words came, "No, I do not know him. How can I know him?"

"Bill, can you be—will you be—childlike enough to simply say 'Lord Jesus, come into my heart. Remove my intellectual doubts. Fill me with thy Spirit. Be Lord of my life'?"

As this man's mask of control gave way to sobs from the depths of his being, I suffered with him. Then I left him so that God might do his mighty work within. Two hours later he sent word he wanted to see me. He wanted to say, "I did ask and He came. Now I *know.*"

The next day at the final hour of sharing, it was quite a different man who walked down to the front of that room to witness to those present. His pride had been shattered, but he was whole. Publicly he thanked God for allowing that to which he had given lip service, that about which he had preached for forty years, to become real within his own experience.

We are a generation of Christians who have come to equate membership in the church with discipleship to Jesus Christ. But one does not necessarily follow the other. We discuss the value of the meditative life, but leave no time to meditate. We'd rather debate the Bible than read it.

If the Bible is to feed us, it is well to remember that we are to take, read, mark, and inwardly digest. Helpful guidelines for reading the Bible devotionally are:

1. Approach the Bible with a sense of expectancy. Know God has a message for you. Let the words come alive within your own experience. Come with

questions, knowing that God who spoke to Moses, to Elijah, to Jesus, will speak a relevant word today.

2. Approach the Bible with an open mind. Often our familiarity with certain scripture deafens us to the truth which needs to be discovered. It is well to come to the Bible each day as if we had never read it before. Come without preconceived notions, without predetermined theology. Open your mind to hear God speak in new ways.

   For many years it was the habit of Dr. Laubach to get a New Testament each year in order to avoid noticing the markings which he had made. In this way he would open himself to new truths each year. A young woman asked if she might purchase a Testament for him to use for a year, after which she would have it. He agreed. At the close of the year when the used Testament was returned, she discovered that almost every word was underscored.

3. Approach the Bible with an open heart. Becoming spiritually sensitive should be a goal of all who claim Jesus as the model for life. The eyes of the heart need enlightenment. How thankful am I that we are beginning to admit we are a feeling people, not just thinking people. The falseness that denies and fears emotions leaves a sterile, cold theology which never heals a broken heart or challenges one to respond.

4. Approach the Bible prayerfully. Ask the Spirit to interpret. Seek the wisdom of Christ who promised to give liberally when asked.

5. Approach the Bible regularly. Daily feeding on the Word is required diet. As the Israelites wandered in the wilderness God provided fresh manna every day.

So must we learn to "taste and see that the Lord is good" daily. Since we are creatures of habit, we need to establish habits appropriate for citizens of heaven.

6. Live with the same scripture until it becomes yours. Many seekers prefer to read and re-read the same scripture rather than rush through the Bible. Seeking fresh insights requires much pondering.

   Estelle Carver first brought this way of reading the Bible to my attention. At that time she was "living with Colossians all year." She read the entire book daily and memorized the major portion. I have discovered as I follow this practice, even for a month, it proves a deepening experience.

7. Memorize scripture. Particularly are the Psalms great for memorization. The passages which have spoken to you can become your own as you commit them to memory, to be recalled at needed moments. A sad lack within most church schools (as well as secular) is the de-emphasis on memorization.

Because many enter kingdom-living in a dramatic way and all life is transfigured by that peak experience, we expect to continue to live at that level. Such is not the case. Peter, James, and John had to learn this grim lesson as Jesus led them from the Mount of Transfiguration down into the valley of discontent. Like Peter, all of us would build booths. We would like to preserve the full glow of a high experience. But such moments are fleeting. We are to walk in the day-by-day routine of life. However, we can so cultivate an awareness of God that even the prosaic, the monotonous, can become aglow with his Spirit.

I remember some weeks after my husband's death when

it seemed as if God, who as the Holy Comforter had carried me so lovingly, suddenly dropped me. No longer was I held in his encircling love. Desolate, I cried out, "Where are You?" His voice came, "I have held you as a tender baby in my loving arms. But I do not want you to remain a baby. You are to mature. Get up and walk by faith, not feeling."

"Thank you, Father," and I picked myself up from the floor.

Newness of life—the life of faith—demands totally new attitudes. God will not let us go until he has rid us of all our old parochialism, all our prejudice, all our negativism. Even our vocabulary has to be revamped. We discover words like *hopeless, impossible, anxious* to be inappropriate for a Christian. We who have thought that a thorough job of worrying indicated the degree of our caring have to learn that anxiety is a sign of distrust of the Father. When I say, "That person can never change," or, "I will always be this way," I am really saying, "This job is too big for God."

Our value system has to undergo complete revision. The words *success* and *failure* are seen in a new light. At a time of crisis in human relations, when the long, hot summer was weighing heavily upon me, I went to a Christian ashram to gain a new perspective. I had a session with Dr. E. Stanley Jones, founder of the ashram movement. I must confess I was hopeful he would counsel me to leave the tension-filled job as executive director of the Commission on Human Relations.

I explained to him that I knew God had placed me in that job. I thought I had matured spiritually to the point of being free to fail. Now, I found myself in the position of hating the fact that I was failing—human relations had worsened. Dr. Jones looked me straight in the eye and said, "Never forget this, Mary Virginia. When you start with Christ, *you start from victory.* You never fail, no matter how things may look to the contrary." Those were the words I needed. Even though I never saw the changes and improvements I had envisioned for the community, I was able to continue with a sense of purpose. I was willing to do my best without any outward sign of success.

Our thought patterns must be altered by a deliberate set of the will. When we gaze on violence, fear and suspicion overtake us, and we are paralyzed. In today's society, we are so bombarded by negative pictures, stories, movies, soap operas, we cannot escape evil thoughts unless we ruthlessly cut them off. Does this mean withdrawal into never-never land? No, but it does mean a determination not to fill our minds with junk food, just as my grandson is not to fill his stomach with what he has been taught to call junk food.

As God's highest creation, we are given the capacity to choose. We choose that which we will dwell upon. I recall one of my first prayers shortly after becoming a widow. "Dear Lord, please do not let me fall captive to the P.L.O.M (poor-little-old-me) syndrome." Self-pity is one of the most enervating and destructive of all human emotions. Like quicksand, it can suck you down into despair within minutes.

The choice is ours—to think on that which pulls us down or that which lifts our thoughts to God and to praise of him. I have found the Psalms extremely helpful in lifting my thoughts Godward. When I am tempted to indulge in self-pity (to which we are all subject), I identify with the psalmist who said with candor, "Out of my distress I called

on the Lord; the Lord answered me and set me free"
(Ps. 118:5). This is the mission of our Lord. What a
glorious discovery!

Spiritual awareness must be cultivated if we would walk
in newness of life. All our senses must find their
counterparts in the spiritual realm. Recently, there was
placed in my hand a little black, two-by-four-inch card on
which was written, "What do you see?" Beneath the
question were some lines and marks which, at first glance,
had no meaning. After a rather frustrating time, my eyes
were able to focus on the word Jesus. Once the name
becomes clear, it is readily seen each time one looks at it.
So it is with the spiritual life. Once the hidden becomes
revealed, our focus is changed. We begin to comprehend
the statement of Jesus, "I only do what I see my Father
doing." More and more am I discovering the creative
power of seeing—seeing God at work, seeing the divine
potential in a person, seeing through the outer to the inner.

Can this spiritual pilgrimage be made alone? Although
there are some walks that must be solitary, one cannot be
fully Christian alone. We need the companionship, the
support of a small, searching, caring group.

"Mary Virginia thinks you just haven't lived unless you
belong to a prayer group." These words were spoken by a
friend. Perhaps I am guilty of being overly enthusiastic
about those things that are meaningful to me. Prayer
groups have provided such supportive help for me, I owe
them my allegiance. Each of us has a great need for
intimacy, yet life seems to be lived out on the level of
superficiality, if not artificiality. A prayer group can offer
opportunity for deeper relationships, and I shall describe

62

one group with which I've shared my life. It was a couples group which met in our home for almost ten years.

After seeing a group of people pray together at my first CFO, I came home all primed to organize a group. Being president of the League of Women Voters, organization was my trademark. I had and have the greatest respect for the league, but a prayer group and the league do not come into being by the same method, or for the same purpose. I had to learn this as I've had to learn most lessons—painfully.

I had asked to sit in on a CFO council ring to see how it was organized. When I noted the difference—those who had learned dependence on God were free from agenda—I came home ready to relinquish my dream of a prayer group and my dream of a Kentucky CFO.

"Just what I wanted," I heard God say. Relinquishment seems to be primary for the movement of God's spirit.

I still don't understand this. Great desire has to be followed by complete relinquishment before his will can be done. Whether I understand it or not, it is his pattern. I don't understand prayer any more than I understand radio or TV or planes, but I'm grateful I have use of them all.

Let me share with you some of the strengths of the prayer group to which I referred.

1. We were drawn together by God, not manipulated into being.
2. We came from different denominational backgrounds.
3. We had diversity of personality—some who kept our feet on the ground, some who raised our sights to the heavens.

4. We shared a mutual hunger to know God at a deeper level and to learn how to pray.
5. We set a minimum discipline:
   a. to have at least a fifteen-minute devotional period daily;
   b. to pray for one another daily;
   c. to be willing to share what God was doing in our lives with the group—needs, hurts, joys, fears;
   d. to be actively engaged in the corporate worship within our own churches.

Small groups should never replace corporate worship. However, within a small group there is built a trust, an intimacy which can never be experienced in a formal worship service. Sharing brings a new liberation. Masks can be removed and one can dare to expose his feelings, to cry without apology, to question without a sense of guilt.

Our group had a common call, to pray into actuality a Kentucky CFO. The surprising way this came about in 1960 indicated a power at work beyond ourselves.

The group, as you would expect, also had some weaknesses.

1. Our knowledge of prayer was limited, but we stumbled and fell together.
2. Our feelings were ambivalent. To keep the group closed seemed so exclusive, but to remain open disrupted the unity each time new members came in. This fact is recognized by those who are skilled in the art of communication.
3. We often failed to recognize the need for individual growth which could take different paths.
4. Our failure to set short-term commitments rather than drag on and on.

Even though we failed in many ways, the strengths more than compensated for the weaknesses. I believe every person would confess a deep indebtedness to that group and a strong continuing love among the persons who comprised it. Certainly, I will be everlastingly grateful for their support.

Creating growth opportunities of a vital, intimate nature is essential. Jesus gave us the classic example. He called together just twelve whom he discipled. Out of that small number, he called three to go aside with him to pray; to share some of the highest moments and some of the most agonizing struggles of his life.

We are a size-oriented society. If we would seek Christian growth, we need to return to the original pattern established by our Master. The fires of church renewal for which we pray can be lit only as individuals become aflame with his Spirit. Through small, caring groups, one learns to kindle and communicate this holy fire. Together, we "may receive that inner illumination of the spirit which will make you realise how great is the hope to which he is calling you—the magnificence and splendour of the inheritance promised to Christians—and how tremendous is the power available to us who believe in God" (Eph. 1:18, 19 Phillips).

Chapter Five

Wilderness Wanderings

I had a dream of being alone on a mountain climb. There were many forks in the trail, and it seemed as if I wandered down each one only to arrive at a dead end or an impenetrable jungle. My discouragement mounted as I went round and round never seeming to come any nearer my goal. I grumbled at ever undertaking such a trek, but from the bottom, I had caught a vision of the peak which beckoned me upward. Now there was no turning back. After endless wanderings, I sighted the top. Were my eyes playing tricks on me? Who was that sitting there so completely "at home"? I neared the summit and saw that, sure enough, it was Mrs. Woodruff, unruffled and serenely calm, as if she'd been there all the time. (Mrs. Woodruff, an elderly saint, was a member of the Woman's Bible Class I was teaching at the time.) When I recovered my breath from the climb, I asked her how she had arrived with no apparent effort or discomfort. Her answer, innocent as a child's, was, "I just kept my hand in the hand of Jesus, and he led me straight up the mountain. When the going got rough, he lifted me over the boulders. It was very simple."

Most of us have to take a more circuitous route. Like the Israelites who, on leaving the bondage of Egypt, had to go through forty years of wilderness wanderings before sighting the Promised Land, which was actually only a few weeks' journey away, we too must take the long way around. There are times of regret at leaving the old, the safe status quo. There are times of fear when the new, the unknown loom frighteningly large. There are periods when the temptation to make other gods is very real and very appealing.

Once loosed from old patterns, we find new attractions tantalizing. So enticing are they that it is easy to "nibble one's self lost," like sheep that go astray. Tired of endless wanderings, one longs for the "good old days." Questions and doubts begin to torment. General discouragement sets in. Things of the world grow more fascinating. One questions whether the promised goal is worth the struggle.

Many of us have the false idea that if we surrender our wills to God, the "land of milk and honey" is instantly ours. Not so. Each of us must spend some time in the wilderness—just how long, may well depend on how quickly we discover and abide by spiritual secrets. The wilderness experiences of Jesus should teach us that there are no shortcuts to spiritual power.

I remember a most unusual episode when, led by the Spirit, I refused to pray as requested. I was visiting with a prayer group at a retreat where I was a speaker. The leader of the group asked if I would pray for the young man who had asked that he might receive more of the Spirit's power. A legitimate request. Yet, I perceived his motives were all wrong. There was much hate in his heart. I refused, and even made the harsh statement that Simon the magician also wanted more power. Understandably angry, the young man started to reveal his true nature. As he poured out his wrath, he finally confessed great hatred for his parents. Then he broke into uncontrollable sobs which ended in his seeking God's forgiveness with the promise he would ask forgiveness from his parents. Once cleansed, he was ready to receive fullness of the Spirit. As we prayed, it was a joy to see the release that took place, not only within that young man, but within others in the group.

My daring to liken him to Simon sent me to the Bible to get better acquainted. My search revealed that Simon had met some of the requirements, but not all. He believed. He was baptized. But Simon was a man whose faith did not end in holiness. His only desire was to evoke amazement, not repentance, obedience, and wholeness. Many of us, like Simon, err in wanting the *power* of Jesus, but not Jesus.

There seems to be a period in each of our pilgrimages when all sense of place is lost. Dr. E. Stanley Jones described this state being halfway between "a worm and a wonder." I remember such a time. Earlier I described my devastating encounter with God when my place was shaken. After that, there were several months when I felt somewhat like a trapeze artist who has let go of one trapeze but has yet to grasp the other. Thank God, I did know his arms, like a net, were beneath.

Today our world is flooded with all sorts of counterfeits and half-truths. We Christians, of all people, must be most aware. No wonder Jesus said we must be wise as serpents. Nibbling one's way lost is quite easy in today's society.

Once we enter the realm of the Spirit, spirits other than the Holy begin to tease. There are many alluring bypaths. Philosophies using similar terminology sound attractive. They speak of the same goals, yet miss the mark completely. We read books written by influential persons and wander where they beckon, wasting precious time, and sometimes losing our way. How innocent the detour seems. We rationalize this diversion as a desire to know other schools of thought. God has placed me in some rather unique situations to show how subtly one can be led away from Jesus who said, "I am the way and the way is narrow."

My first bypath was the exploration of reincarnation. I found it a fascinating philosophy and sought God's revelation. Is this contrary to the Christian faith? I had to have a firsthand encounter with the sister of a leader in this movement, and that allowed God to show me the falseness of the Eastern philosophy of reincarnation. When this woman related to me her struggle and her despair of ever reaching the final state of perfection, a compassion beyond my own welled up within me. I said, "But Miss———, what about grace?" It was the first time I recall ever using that word, and it was the first time grace had real meaning.

As the words were said through me I was given a picture, a ladder with a tired, elderly woman (who, according to her belief, had lived through many lifetimes) struggling to reach the top, always out of reach for it was nowhere. To the upper right of the ladder was Jesus, reaching down with hand outstretched, inviting her to let him who is the pioneer and perfecter of our faith, lift her into the heavenlies. So glued were her eyes to the rungs of the

69

ladder that she missed the outstretched hand. For me, this was God's answer to my prayer, "Teach me thy truth."

Persons consult astrologers rather than the Scriptures. Many see no inconsistency in following philosophies introduced through Eastern religions. Many are now being led into witchcraft and the occult. Witches are no longer the imaginary creatures in ghost stories who ride brooms. I was completely amazed recently to meet and talk for three hours with a young man who had been a priest for a coven of witches in one of our leading cities. During the same weekend, I met a young man from the House of Satan.

It is at such times that I would love to run back to the safety of my childhood. But once we have been pushed out, there is no turning back. We begin to get glimpses of the very real battle that is being waged in our day for the minds and hearts of people, particularly the young. Much of what they are being taught defeats them. Life becomes meaningless, and that accounts for suicide's being the second highest cause of death among the young in our nation.

How apropos are the words of Paul,

Be careful that nobody spoils your faith through intellectualism or high-sounding nonsense. Such stuff is at best founded on men's ideas of the nature of the world and disregards Christ! Yet it is in him that God gives a full and complete expression of himself in bodily form. Moreover, your own completeness is only realised in him, who is the ruler over all authorities, and the supreme power over all powers. (Col. 2:8-10 Phillips)

An outstanding Christian author asked me to read and comment on her book about a psychic whose feats truly dazzle the mind. This was a strange request for I did not know the writer, nor have I ever met her. Her fascinating volume was being discussed by many. The bizarre always draws a crowd, and this book was the in thing.

I was aware of my inability to judge such a book, and I earnestly sought the wisdom of God as to the truth about spiritualism. As I searched the mind of Jesus, these words came loud and clear, "Let me be your control." (*Control* is the term given the intermediary.) For me, this was the truth. Jesus is the only one in the unseen world we are to seek. I wrote the author of God's direction to me.

I fully realized what a dangerous exploration this could be, since my baby had died shortly after birth. What if I were to seek and receive a request from that child? Would my sentimental maternalism want to respond? I answered my unknown friend's request, sharing some of these thoughts and also the very clear direction of Jesus, "Let me be your control." When she replied with a seven-page letter defending her position of seeking wisdom and God's will through mediums rather than through Jesus, it confirmed my guidance, for truth needs no defense.

I have a growing understanding of the words "I, thy God, am a jealous God" as I see countless young people being led into false teachings. My initial encounter with such confusion was at a leading college where I was serving as a CFO speaking leader. A student, Rob, who was attending classes on the campus heard some of the talks. Something I said aroused his interest, and he asked for an appointment.

It was a strange meeting. His face and body were so immobile that even his eyelids showed no sign of life. He was so unresponsive that when I asked his name, his only reply was, "Does it matter?" It is certainly difficult to communicate with a person who has disciplined his body and his mind to almost total insensibility. Hypnotic were his eyes, sunken into pools of darkness. If ever I have looked into emptiness, it was within him. As I try to describe him, a cardboard man is the only portrait that would give an inkling of his condition.

As I sought to evoke some response, I learned he had been caught up first in transcendental meditation, then yoga. His unvoiced plea for help tugged at my heart. All that week I, along with the several hundred persons at CFO, prayed and yearned over him.

On the last day of camp Rob and I had a two-hour session, and I related to him the Christian message of which he seemed totally ignorant. Finally, as I spoke of the love of Jesus for him, even His willingness to die on a cross for him, there came a breakthrough. The immobile face broke. The lips began to quiver and a verbal acceptance of Jesus was made. He was, at least temporarily, filled with His Spirit. He told me, "All the darkness is breaking up." This was apparent to those who saw him enter the dining room with a glow upon his face.

Regretfully, the story from this point on is not joyous. Without continuing instruction, he was an easy prey for the young guru who has influenced thousands of our young people. My friend submitted to him and his teachings. When I learned of this, I tried to point out the error, but he could not see it, for the guru used the same words—love, peace, light, truth, brotherhood—and even quoted the Scriptures. My young friend, not being rooted and grounded in scripture, could not distinguish between the truth as revealed in the person of Jesus and the teaching of the guru.

After following the guru for eighteen months, my friend

was in despair. He called and asked if he might come and see me for several days. This he did, traveling over 1100 miles. When I saw his confusion, I knew his mind would have to be completely reprogrammed. I asked him, "Why would an intelligent young man like you follow a young guru who was so obviously using you for personal gain?" The reply came, "I would have followed anybody who *really believed in something.* He promised to lead me in discovering universal truth."

While my friend spoke, using the same terminology Christians often use, I sought God's wisdom as to the difference. The reply was, "So long as one searches for universals—love, truth, brotherhood—they will not be found. If one seeks and is found by Jesus, the *Person,* he brings all these to the seeker."

It is my prayer that we who follow the Christ may become alert to the battle being waged for the minds and hearts of young intellectuals. May we be equipped to encounter and overcome the enemies of darkness prevalent in our day.

Very few of us are confronted by gurus. We may not build golden calves and fall down in worship, yet we need to recognize that the force in which we place our trust becomes our god. Is it materialism? Is it military might? Is it technology? Is it a technique which has captured our attention?

Are we wandering aimlessly in the wilderness? Have we forgotten our original destination? Have we become confused in the maze of bypaths?

Have we ignored the voice of God who said, "Thou shall have no other gods before me?" Are our ears and hearts attuned to the One who said, "I am the way"?

Chapter Six

Discoveries and Disclosures

My husband used to say that I was never so happy as when I had everybody working. What a happy day for me when I discovered that *God* is at work. How foolish that statement sounds, yet we live out our lives as if we didn't believe it. Admit it or not, our behavior patterns, our policy-making, even our church business indicate we think God has abdicated and is totally dependent on us.

How exciting the journey becomes as discoveries and disclosures are made. To discover that the One you seek is seeking you; that the One you choose has already chosen you; that the Way anticipated is already revealed. This truly is the joy of the Lord. When mere words become alive as the Word, when truth sought for years is imparted, a new song is on our lips. We discover why the message is good news for every man. As God reveals himself, we enter into a new relationship. The Father of our Lord Jesus becomes our Father. Sonship is ours and family secrets are shared.

Our discoveries are his disclosures. God is the initiator.

DISCOVERIES AND DISCLOSURES

The secret hidden through the ages is made known, and we are in on it. Wonder of wonders! God is real, not the figment of someone's imagination, not a myth handed down from generation to generation. He is not far away and unapproachable. He is here, and he is knowable.

We give lip service to the omnipresent God, yet we really think of him as being only in special places—the church sanctuary, the prayer room, the dwelling of the saint. So, it came as a surprise to me to find him in city hall.

After my husband's death, I prayed for a job with a challenge. I did not mean as much challenge as I got, but then, it's always dangerous to pray. God directed me to city hall. ("Surely, Lord, there must be a mistake. Don't you want me as a prayer leader or in some 'spiritual' job? City hall? Am I hearing you correctly?") All my usual checks for guidance said city hall.

Since I had had no previous public career, I felt like a first-grader on my initial day at work. Frightened and unsure, I entered the municipal building still with much questioning directed Godward. I stopped to introduce myself to the operator on the switchboard. I looked at the book she was reading. It couldn't be. Glenn Clark's *I Will Lift Up Mine Eyes*. If God had sent to me, as he did to Jacob, a ladder with angels ascending and descending, it could not have been a clearer sign. "I am here. You are in the place of my choosing."

There is no such thing as coincidence for a Christian. When this truth became my own, I stepped into a new level of consciousness. Every experience, every belief I held had to be reexamined in the light of this fact. The scripture that had caused me much agony of soul became meaningful, "We know that in everything God works for

75

good with those who love him, who are called according to his purpose" (Rom. 8:28). As I began to look at all the circumstances of life from this new perspective, I could see God at work in his wonderfully creative way. His ability to manipulate situations was brought to my attention with dramatic impact through the following event.

Tired after a tour of the Orient and anticipating a restful night on the flight from Honolulu to Los Angeles, I prepared to go through customs with two of my sisters who were my traveling companions. We were happily surprised when the man in charge of the Pan American flight asked if we would like to fly first class. We thanked him and said yes. I had been seated only a short time when the stewardess came and asked me to move across the aisle and back one row. Though puzzled by the request, I was happy to comply.

There came onto the plane a most disheveled young man. Half-drunk, cursing and angry at life, he was helped into the seat next to me by the same man who had suggested our change to first class. As I looked at the newcomer—the epitome of offensiveness—I thanked God he had removed the scales from my eyes to see beyond the exterior. I saw beneath the beard, I heard beyond the words a cry for help.

When he turned to me and said, "You're stuck with me as a seatmate all the way to L.A." I looked at him and said, "So I see. Tell me, what is so terribly wrong?"

This was his story. Only three hours before he had been notified from Los Angeles that one of his five-year-old twin boys had drowned. Not knowing how to handle his grief, he was trying to escape through drunkenness. He was angry at friends who had said, "I know how you feel."

With an oath, he said, "But they don't know how I feel. They have never lost a son."

"But I have," was my reply.

He accepted me as one who could identify with his grief. However, I realized I must keep my silence. A few questions revealed he had not only lost a son, but he did not know a heavenly Father. He had been disillusioned while attending seminary, and he went into public-relations work. I sought to determine his relationship with God. It became evident he was a humanist: Man is all there is; man is sufficient. Now, he found that he was *not* sufficient, and he had nowhere to turn.

How desperately lonely and frightened he was. He said he would not get off the plane—he knew he could not face his wife who was suffering not only the sorrow, but also guilt for not having been more watchful of the boys. In his desperation, Chip would beat on the back of the seat in front of us. Angry at his own inadequacy, he was almost suicidal in his speech and in his actions. When he left the seat even for a short time, I was fearful for him.

In between his outbursts, we talked of many things. I discovered the beard was new, grown while making repairs on a home which he had up for sale. He had a prominent position in Hawaii, but his family had health problems which instigated the move back to California. I discovered that he was a brilliant young man, a concerned, sensitive person. The sleep I had envisioned was forgotten as I related to this young man who was so deeply hurt. I knew God had engineered my being there to identify with his sorrow.

I respected Chip's request for no sermonizing. However, that did not stop my inward prayer for him. Every so often, he would turn, look me straight in the eye and say, "What are you doing to me?" "Nothing, why?" "I feel as if you were boring a hole through my head." I knew my prayers were having some effect.

Periodically, he would say, "You know, you are a *real* person." I knew that was his way of saying, "Thank you for caring."

All night long I respected his right to curse God, to scream out that there was no God, but one hour out of Los Angeles when he was becoming increasingly nervous over the prospect of having to meet his wife, of having to fulfill a role of strength which he did not have, I took his hand and said, "Chip, I've listened to you the whole night through. Now you are going to listen to me. I know the agony of your heart and the awful inward pain. I know the many questions haunting you. But I also know there is a God who loves you. I know there is a God who can strengthen you. You don't believe in God or in prayer, but I do. And now, you are going to listen to me beseech God to come into you and give you the strength to walk off this plane like a man to comfort your wife and your son. Even though you are at the end of your strength, God says, 'I'm here. My strength is made perfect in your weakness.'" And I prayed. Oh, how I prayed. I could almost feel God's strength entering him and with it, a great calm.

When I last saw Chip, he was a sobered young man meeting his father, patting him on the shoulder, and putting his arm around him as together, they walked up the ramp into the airport. And I thought, "There goes God's man."

How wonderfully loving is our God. He engineers circumstances so that the people he can use will be in the right places at the right time. Three times he moved me, but nothing is too much trouble for God.

To a Christian, there *is* no such thing as coincidence. What a difference that makes. What a relief to be able to look at everything and know that God has planned it all—the circumstances we are in, the people we meet, the job at hand. No longer do we think in terms of luck or out-of-the-blue happenings. God is in it all. *God is all.* Praise his holy name.

As he discloses himself—his *is*-ness, his *here*-ness, his *all*-ness—we begin to discover some of the secrets hidden from those who do not seek. Most of us have real difficulty discerning God's guidance. How often we say or hear, "I would be willing to do God's will if only I knew it." Would we? I have come to believe that if I'm willing to do his will, I'll know it.

How does God guide? I am often asked, "How can I tell his voice from my own thoughts?" If I am centered in him, I have to assume that my inner urges are his guidance (provided, of course, they are in keeping with the character of God). The way he guides me most frequently is through promptings to call a person, write a note, or speak a word. If this feeling persists, and I ask that he block any impulse which is not of him, then I know that he wants to use my voice, my pen, my call to speak his word. So amazing have been some responses, I would certainly hesitate to ignore the nudges.

I recall a certain afternoon when I had a strong sense of urgency to call a young minister whom I knew very slightly. I tried to dismiss the thought and continue with my work, but it persisted. I had no message to give him and felt a bit of a fool, but I followed my guidance by calling him long distance and saying, "It seems that God is telling me to call you and ask if you have a special need." He was deeply moved with gratitude for he had been going through a period of depression and at that particular moment was in real despair. The call let him know that he had a Father who cared for him. Later, he wrote that his reassurance of God's love through that call lifted his gloom and restored his faith.

Sometimes, we are guided to speak a word which may have no meaning for us but will for the recipient. I remember such an occasion when a woman suffering from some throat disorder asked me to pray for her. I laid my hands on her throat and heard myself praying, "Lord, free her from all resentments." Never having seen the woman before, my words came as a surprise to me and, certainly, to her. They brought forth sobbing as she confessed that she had felt resentment toward her mother for years. She sought forgiveness from God and from her mother, and in the process, was healed—emotionally and physically. Sometimes God grants us the gift of discernment, but sometimes we are only guided to speak the word given. He blesses and brings results.

His guidance is revealed in three ways: (1) The Scriptures are the primary way. How we need to soak in the Scriptures; to be so acquainted with them that they become our handbook for every question, every problem, every decision. We need to make a habit of going to the Bible seeking God's word for our particular need. (2) God guides directly. Prayer becomes continuous conversation whether in the closet, in the street, or in the marketplace; and he will impress upon our minds and hearts his will. (3) God guides through circumstances. People and situations which we meet reveal what he wants of us. We do not have to struggle to be somewhere else. We do not even have to resent interruptions during our carefully planned days. We must only listen and respond to his gentle nudgings.

If one has a decision to make which involves major changes, it is wise to wait until three things come into focus: God's impressions within; God's word without; God's providence ("circumstances") around. Once a secret is revealed, one wonders why it took so long to find it. As we become established, that is, rooted and grounded in him, we may not have the mountaintop experience, yet we become more constant in our awareness of him. How does one maintain that awareness? Through obedience.

Obedience is the key to spiritual understanding. God's revelation will not be opened by philosophy or mental gymnastics. Immediately you obey, a flash of light comes, and you have new insight into his nature.

Having a great sense of the dramatic, the heroic, I have had to be taught patiently by God of his concern for all life—not just those things we think of as high and holy. No area of life is outside his dominion when we make him Lord. Once God reveals the fact of his atonement as the foundation on which all his sons can live, obedience becomes a spontaneous response. When we say *yes* to him, God moves heaven and earth to provide.

For the last several years, God has been working on me in the area of his security, economically. As the "old me," I could not believe some of the stories told by speakers and writers of the way in which money seemed to flow to them at just the right time. But God has shown me that my attitude was unbelief in his almightiness. When we seek to

live in obedience to his will, ever letting him reveal more
and more of himself, we discover he is perfectly capable of
meeting our needs.

This was first brought home to me in this way. I was
planning to go to a retreat as a camper, which meant it
would cost me $100.00. On the basis of obedience to Him,
I sent in the registration, even though I inwardly
questioned the expenditure. The day before camp, I again
sought the Lord's guidance and his answer was go.

In the mail that day, I had a letter from a couple who had
attended a retreat I led for the Protestant Women of the
Chapel in Fort Leavenworth, Kansas. The wife wrote that
God had blessed her husband at that retreat and that he
felt led by God to send me a gift to be used any way I
wished. When I unfolded the enclosed check, it was for
one hundred dollars. Sometimes, God waits until the
eleventh hour to supply, but supply he will, not only
revealed truth, but such mundane, worldly—yet
necessary—things as money. What an amazing Father we
have!

Obedience may demand that we do the hard thing—
that we ask forgiveness of someone who has wronged us;
that we appear in a role which is unpopular; that we
witness to a group who make us feel as if we had lost our
mind. But disobedience means that communication is
severed, relationship with the Father is broken, His
revelation is ended . . . and that is what is known as hell.

Thanksgiving and praise open the channels to God.
"Just keep thanking him. That's the way the blessings
come." This truth was given me by a black friend when I
said, "Martha, I thank God for the many kindnesses Ann
Carter and I have received since Cliff's death. God is truly

good." Then she gave me the sage advice, and I have found it true. How he honors our thanks and praise! If you find yourself somewhat depressed and indulging in a bit of self-pity, may I recommend Martha's secret, "Just keep thanking him. That's the way the blessings come."

Space, stillness, and solitude are needed by every seeker. It took the second heart attack for me to get the message. I was doing the Lord's work, but not in the Lord's way. I should have learned after the first attack, for he gave me a scripture. "In returning and rest you shall be saved; in quietness and in trust shall be your strength" (Isa. 30:15). It was gracious of God not to allow me to know the last part of that verse for it says, *"And you would not."*

I can thank God for that period of inactivity when I looked at the pattern of my life from a new perspective. I had to confess that I was so busy "working for God," I was not allowing him to do his mighty work through me. How easy it is to run ahead and call back over our shoulders, "Bless my efforts, Lord."

Japanese flower arrangements had always seemed sparse to me until I was in Japan and watched an artist arrange a bouquet. As she intrepreted the symbolic meaning of each branch, I saw with new eyes the use of space. It was not emptiness, but a planned part of the whole. By contrast, how cluttered our lives seem. We are uncomfortable with space or silence, and we rush to fill it with activity and sound.

After my heart attacks when I had no visitors, the periods of isolation taught me a new quietness. It was preparation for living alone as a widow. I have discovered that being alone can mean the agony of loneliness or the joy of solitude. The choice is always ours. "Be still and know that

I am God" becomes meaningful as we make space in our busy lives for quiet reflection upon him.

Do these discoveries, these disclosures help one to deal with the day-by-day problems, with fear, with anger, with frustration? I have found they do. As I've learned to depend on God, have sought his direction no matter what the circumstance, I have found him always faithful. Let me share with you a specific frustration which I experienced just last year.

The week of CFO was almost over. As I prepared for my last two talks, it seemed as if I were flooded with thoughts which cried for expression.

I was ready for the evening talk, but the preceding event went on and on. A restlessness was growing within the audience and within me. Some persons had driven from a neighboring town to hear me speak. As the hour grew late, I felt that no one should be required to listen to a talk at such an hour. So, it was canceled. Like a race horse primed to run a race, I felt cheated and disquieted.

The next morning I was to attempt to combine both talks into my last message to that group I had grown to love during the week. Eager to get started and not miss a moment, again I found another event—a very important one—had been scheduled, and my talk was delayed half an hour. But, a half-hour, an hour, two hours passed before the group returned from the baptismal service. The talk would be canceled, and I was to speak that evening. This meant that Bob Forbes, the other speaker, would be cut out of one talk. This I did not like.

It had been a long time since I had felt such anger, such frustration. I knew I needed to go to the privacy of my room and closet myself with the Lord until I was acceptable company. I have to admit it took many hours, but the Lord taught me a lot. This was my instruction from him:

1. Write out exactly how you feel, don't deny your feelings. Don't feel guilty. After all, you are just a human, remember? Be honest. Acknowledge that you are terribly mad. Be real, even if you are supposed to be the spiritual leader. Wrestle with your anger, recognizing there are alternative ways of responding.

2. Get out all the anger. Keep writing until all your anger is spent in a nondestructive way through verbalization—on paper—in private. Repressed anger will come back to haunt you and will erupt in very inappropriate ways and at very inconvenient times.

3. Don't hate yourself for being angry about the baptismal service, which you know to be more important than your little talk. Know that you'll always have frustrations; you'll always have tribulations. But, be of good cheer, for I have overcome the world, and I give you the power to manifest my victory.

4. Think on Psalm 139. Read it over and over aloud until you are looking at everything from a different viewpoint.

I followed God's direction, even to missing a meal for he said I should not eat while so angry. As I thought on the psalm to which I was drawn, my prayers changed from self-centeredness to thanksgiving. How thankful I was that God would listen as long as it required. He wouldn't look at any clock and say, "Time's up. Come again next week." He patiently loved me into a willingness to forgive others and myself.

He gave me the strength to get up before those people gathered that evening and confess my great anger. I could have acted with a false smile, but I chose to let them know what I had learned—that out of the same mouth can come words of anger and words given by God. We are never more than a container of his divinity, and I knew better than to dare speak in his name without his Spirit.

With fresh insight, we discover the interplay between God and man. We appreciate the real meaning of the term "earthen vessels." How gracious of God to allow us to share in the manifestation of his power; though we must remember always that the transcendent power belongs to him. We rejoice that he wants us in on the act. To him be the glory, for ever and ever. Amen.

Chapter Seven

Simplification of Life

We are not meant to be divided selves; we are not made to live compartmentalized lives. God destined us for holiness (wholeness). Most of our lives are like mixed-up puzzles without design. We have no mental image of what life is meant to be. We have forgotten who we are and from whom we come and to whom we belong.

Our difficulty comes from our failure to see life whole. We live many lives (wear many hats), we make many laws, we serve many lords. If we would avoid the complexity that is so much a part of today's society, if we would discover life's secret, we need to simplify life.

The growing realization that there is only one life in the universe has helped me see beyond separatism and brokenness to unity. Jesus who is life spoke of the vine and the branch. He said, "Apart from me you can do nothing at all" (John 15:5 Phillips). Our lives are meant to be extensions of his life. There was no disunity in the life of our Lord—he had no worry about the secular versus the

87

sacred. He was one with the Father. Until we become aware of, and receptive to, the life he manifests and offers, we will remain separated persons.

When Jesus said, "Inasmuch as you do it to the least of these, you do it to me, and inasmuch as you do it not to the least of these, you do it not to me," he was using no figure of speech. He meant exactly that. Each of us is designed to be a participant in the one life. Each of us is a tiny drop without which the whole world thirsts. If one is hurt, all suffer; if one is cut, all bleed.

To see wholeness when only brokenness is apparent requires the gift of imagination. Many have discarded this treasure that is given to all. Many have belittled it and feared it, for to some, it connotes fantasy. Yet, it is a godlike quality. Our Bible tells us God made us in his own image—he visualized us and we are.

Our prayer life can never become truly effective until we cultivate an ability to "see" persons and conditions whole. This is not escapism I am advocating; it is not a denial of fact. It is to see with the eyes of Jesus who looked at Simon—the wavering, vacillating Simon—and saw him as Peter, the rock, which he did become.

Somehow, this "seeing through" is hard to describe, yet, there is strange power in it. It goes beyond an analysis of causes to the source of all life and order. Once we mentally fight through the jungle of confusion to this clearing, we are really able to see, and our lives have meaning. When we view other persons through these spiritual lenses, release comes and they are set free. In a sense, we become their liberators.

Such power is the possession of each of us if we but appropriate it. What a responsibility! What a challenge!

Most of our prayers are ineffective because we pray for peace and think (see) war; we pray for healing and think (see) disease. We pray for liberated persons, yet continue to see them imprisoned.

To be given a picture of God's plan creates divine discontent, for always there is the contrast between what appears and what is. In trying to share this, it often comes across as judgmentalism when judgmentalism is not intended.

I can recall such an experience. I was speaking to the Ministerial Association on relationships. They had expected me to confine my remarks to black-white relations, but God would not allow me to stop there. He forced me to speak of the tragedy of the divisions among the churches and of the prayer of Jesus that they may all be one.

It came across as judgmentalism, and I was so angry with God that I lashed out at him for always making me say the unpopular word. I rushed home, and I cried, as is the special privilege of women. But my tears were soon stopped by a long-distance call from a stranger inviting me to serve as retreat co-leader at Yokefellow Center, Earlham College. It was God's loving way of saying, "Don't feel sorry for yourself. You were obedient, and being misunderstood is part of the pain of obedience."

Labels confine and hurt. Seeing through to wholeness releases. Consider this contrast. While conversing with a black friend in my office, he mentioned an incident that had taken place the day before. He was walking down Main Street with his fifteen-month-old daughter in his arms. In her typically warm, outgoing manner, she reached out in friendship to a woman coming down the street.

When he felt his child draw back in fear and start to cry, he looked and saw still on the face of the white woman a look of disdain and disgust.

The first time I met Dr. Laubach I watched in amazement at the change which came over persons' faces as they talked with him. Eager to learn his secret, I asked, "When persons are talking with you, what do you do that makes their expressions change?" Quite surprised at that observation, he answered, "I only pray for them and love them." What a difference it would make if we would learn to listen with such an attitude.

Jesus taught and demonstrated the secret. He simplified the whole legal system of Judaism when he took one law from Leviticus and one from Deuteronomy and joined them together. When asked about the most important laws by the scribe who was attempting to trap him, he answered, "The first is, 'Hear, O Israel: The Lord our God, the Lord is one; and you shall love the Lord your God with all your heart, and with all your soul, and with all your mind, and with all your strength.' The second is this, 'You shall love your neighbor as yourself'" (Mark 12:29-31).

The primacy of the love of God is significant. Jesus knew that if our relationship to the Father was one of reckless devotion, all other relationships would be loving. The all-ness of his demand stumps us. The no-strings-attached type of love is different from our usual conditional love.

Abandonment to God opens the door to receive his limitless love. Then, we are able to love ourselves and others. Our dilemma and despair come from being commanded to love and knowing that we can't. For, we cannot give what we do not have. Hence, God's plan—we can love because God first loved us.

SIMPLIFICATION OF LIFE

Strangely enough, of the three—God, self, others—it seems that a healthy love of self is the most difficult. We have been programmed to think that denying self means hating self. All sorts of guilt and false humility crowd in and hinder our sense of worth. This was not the love message of Jesus.

Psychology has taught us much regarding emotional damage when there is an absence of love. To love self means to accept self. God thinks man is of worth, so who are we to question?

It seems that we need to get our trust in the proper place. We read in the Scriptures that Jesus trusted no man, yet he was never cynical, never despairing. His trust was based on the almightiness of the Father who transforms persons and situations.

In an effort to love the sinner, we have developed an attitude of "anything goes." We confuse the sin with the sinner. It has taken a psychiatrist to bring up the question, Whatever happened to sin? Loving does not imply the acceptance of any and all behavior as OK. To love means to believe in a person, not because of his inherent goodness, but because of his divine potential.

Yet, the fact remains, some people are very hard to love. How does one love the unlovable? Estelle Carver's suggestion is to see F-W-C-D written across their foreheads. If you are like me, I had to ask the meaning of the letters—"for whom Christ died." I confess, when that is remembered, it makes loving easier.

To believe in a person is to create him; to despair of a person is to destroy him. Therefore, we need to eliminate words such as "hopeless" and "impossible" from our thinking. We must learn the difference in godly love (*agape*) and human love, the difference in loving and liking. We like those whose company we enjoy, whose interests and concerns we share. Though not required to like everyone, we are commanded to love everyone. Thank God who provides the love.

God is wonderfully patient. Like Thomas, I needed to see with my own eyes that we do not live isolated lives. Through my years in the field of human relations, I was shown how interwoven are our lives, how our attitudes affect one another. A demonstration of the power of love was given me through the following experience.

It was the week before Christmas. I was preparing my weekly radio program. Although usually I followed an interview format, this program was to be a message about love and human relations. As I typed, the impact of the Christmas story upon me was great. My mind wandered to Mary and the strange choice God made when he chose her to be the mother of the Savior of the world. In my imagination, I saw the humble scene. Why had not God called forth all the trumpeters of heaven? Why had he not made an impressive production of the royal birth? Why did he choose such a lowly way of entering the world? Not at all as I would have arranged it.

As I pondered the mystery of his choice, an even greater wonderment filled me. Not only was he willing to be conceived and brought forth in obscure surroundings to a peasant girl named Mary, but he was willing—even desired—to be born in me. How could this be?

While continuing to type and meditate, the drama of the Incarnation overwhelmed me. I was filled with a love such as I had never experienced. While filled with this indescribable love, I looked up to see a most hostile young man walk through my open office door. His anger increased as he discovered that I was white. No doubt my sex added to my being a suitable target for his hatred. I turned from my typewriter, offered him my hand, invited him to sit and tell me his complaint. This he did for one and a half hours in language to which I was most unaccustomed.

Somehow, it was almost as if the encounter were being acted out before me. Aware of the tremendous love that had filled me, aware of the hatred that he felt, I knew I was observing the age-old drama of love versus hate. It was a strange experience.

I listened to him in silence. As the poison erupted from him, a tremendous love poured out through me to him. Somehow, I knew I was seeing him through the eyes of Christ. I saw all his anger redirected into creative energy. I envisioned his great capacity for constructive leadership.

I could recall the way I might have reacted to his behavior at one time, yet there was no such impulse now. I felt no need to "straighten him out," to defend the rights of others, or even to counsel him. I only listened and loved. I was interested in the outcome of the drama. Would love or hate win? To be so involved, yet so uninvolved, was quite unique.

It came as a surprise to me that I didn't even resent the fact that I would have to stay an extra hour to finish my work. When his anger was spent and he began to think of himself in a new way, he stood, thanked me for my helpfulness, received my "have a blessed Christmas," and left.

When I returned to my typewriter to conclude my radio script, the Christmas message was, "*Love is* more powerful than hate." Only as God's love is transmitted through persons can the hate of the world be absorbed. Is that what is meant by the taking on or the filling up of the suffering of Jesus?

Within that two-hour span, God taught me many lessons. How firmly he implanted within me the fact that ultimately, love will win out. He showed me that I must be willing to be an absorber of hate—no justifying my position, no defensiveness, no cry of inner resentment, "Why take your hate out on me; I never saw you before?" God showed me that I was a part of the reason for the young man's hatred; I shared in the cause of the long-repressed resentment that had to erupt.

God showed me how very important nonverbal communication is. My thoughts had been conveyed to the angry young man, my attitude of love rather than of retaliation had a therapeutic effect upon him. As I saw him with new eyes, I helped him to have a new self-concept. He became a person of worth. He no longer had to hate himself or me.

Another incident spoke to me of love. It was during the blitz in Vietnam, Christmas 1972. I was visiting my daughter and her family in Guam, where my son-in-law, a doctor, was serving his military stint at Andersen Air Force Base. Looking forward to spending a quiet Christmas on a South Pacific island with my children, I was troubled to find that the B-52s based at Andersen were not on their usual "milk run" to Vietnam, but were actively engaged in what seemed to me senseless bombings. The tension on the island increased as thousands of TDYs were flown in. Even Bob Hope's Christmas show failed to relieve the pall which hung over that base.

SIMPLIFICATION OF LIFE

My position was most uncomfortable. Intellectually, I am a pacifist, yet I have never been tested to know how far that ideology will stretch. For me, the constant vibration and noise of those bombers leaving the base every half hour were painful reminders of how contrary was military might to the power of love. I agonized through the nights. In whom did our nation trust? In what? Could we make any claim to being a nation under God?

I read and re-read the scripture account of Jesus weeping over Jerusalem that they might know the things that make for peace. I wept with him and sought his help. He gave me surcease by letting me know that not until our nation humbled itself, not until our nation worshiped him and placed their trust in his supreme power would we know peace. He gave me assurance of his presence, his yearning over our nation, his waiting for intercessors.

Some months after my return from the Orient, I had a visit from a young Marine captain. I was surprised to learn he had been stationed in Thailand during the blitz and was a pilot of one of the fighter planes which met the B-52s and led them to their targets. As I listened to him and observed the tiredness of his young face, my heart was stabbed when he said to me, "Surely, there must be a better way."

These same words were echoed by a young Rhodes scholar I interviewed. He shared with me that he had been visiting friends in Europe during that time. He, too, was puzzled and pained by the action of his nation. His conversation ended with the words, "Surely, there must be a better way."

Each time these words were spoken, my mind went back to the words of Paul when he said, "And I will show you a still more excellent way," before launching into that famous love chapter in First Corinthians 13.

Is the truly personal universal? As only one, can that one make a difference? I believe so. Under the guise of humility, let us not underestimate the power of one life. One plus God equals a majority.

Our problem is an inner one. We forget the invisible precedes the visible. We work at externals thinking if we get them in order, our lives will be less frantic. We dream of South Sea islands, yet when we get there, there is no peace.

We are not integrated persons because we have no center. We have no absolutes. We have no one lord. Our fragmentation comes from our reaching out in many directions. We attempt to respond to every voice, every call. We pride ourselves on the many things we can accomplish, the many committees we are on, the many meetings we attend. We complain about our limited time at home with our families—limitations sometimes caused by meetings for discussing what is wrong with family life. We are torn apart because we have never learned to say no without such a sense of guilt that weariness and frustration are preferable.

The early Christians' one creed was, "Jesus is Lord." How simplified life becomes when Jesus is our only audience, when his "well done" is more treasured than all the awards man can give. Our obedience to him opens our eyes to see the truth, "No one can serve two masters" (Matt. 6:24), and "He who has the Son has life; he who has not the Son of God has not life" (I John 5:12).

As one becomes aware of his reality, life has meaning and the bits and pieces of life come into focus. Jesus is not only a way of life. He is life. The realization dawns, I was dead. Now I live and the life I now live, I live by faith in Jesus who is life.

It is gloriously true. There is one life, one law (love), one Lord.

Chapter Eight

Getting It All Together

"Don't mix your religion with human relations" was the advice given me by a minister friend as I entered city hall. Since I was confident God had opened that door for me, should I ignore him or the minister?

"You pray and I'll work" were the words of a friend when I shared with her the supportive help of a prayer group. "You verbalize your faith. As for me, I'll just let my life be my witness." Which side must I take? To whose voice must I listen? Must I choose one in preference to the other?

How polarized are positions today, and not just in those areas concerning racial issues. We have the humanist as opposed to the Christian, the evangelical as opposed to the liberal, the charismatic as opposed to the traditional. If God is one and we are one, how does it all fit together? This has been a paramount question as I have observed the contemporary scene.

Starting life as a liberal social activist with a vision of

wholeness, I tried in a limited way to "help" God bring his kingdom on earth. Any organization, any group, or movement that seemed to foster a "united" effort, an ecumenical endeavor, won my support and energy. My utopian dreams had to be destroyed before God allowed me to glimpse the reality of his kingdom on earth—a kingdom not made or established by men. Most of us have to suffer both personal and social disillusionment before we are open to his plan. When our dreams are not consistent with his dream, when our methods conflict with his method, they must be shattered before we begin to see the whole picture.

Man-made programs always end in futility. At one time, I thought enough energy coupled with a spirit of high reform could change the world. I have been actively engaged in consultations on church union, mental health programs, social projects established for the purpose of bringing wholeness and healing. All have served useful purposes; all have been sounding boards against which people could act and react. However, despite good intentions and high hopes, the fact remains that the world still stands in drastic need of change.

When I entered city hall as "ambassador of reconciliation," I had to examine the basis for my strivings. Was my motivation prompted by a secret desire to "save the world"? To change people? Do external changes bring solutions to problems? What is the answer to today's fragmented society?

I have had to learn that there *is a difference* between giving a cup of water and giving a cup of water *in His name,* at His instigation, in His spirit of love. In every area it seems God has led me back to seeing our external (social) problems as internal.

In the process, I think I have discovered why most of us are subconsciously afraid to pray. If we wait long enough for dialogue, God can make us quite miserable. So, we call monologue—simply telling God our desires—prayer.

"You are the only person I've ever seen who uses God as a psychiatrist" was the comment of Howard, a young Jewish friend who had just earned his master's degree in psychology. Never had I thought of prayer in that light before, but I have to admit that when I give God a listening ear, he will bring to my attention various things that need dealing with whether they be honesty of motive, healing from past hurt, or forgiveness from guilt.

An experience of God's pinpointing of motives came when I was serving as speaker at a Camp Farthest Out at Green Lake, Wisconsin. When you spend a week bathed in prayer, God has an opportunity to get in a word now and then. He let me know that the human relations job against which I was inwardly rebelling at the time, was his answer to my childhood prayer. What prayer, I inquired? He reminded me that years before, when our church had had its last "old-fashioned" revival, I had signed a card commiting myself to be a missionary to Africans. Now, I was—only not in Africa, but in Hopkinsville.

God's sense of humor can be rather cutting at times. I had forgotten all about that commitment. Once or twice before reaching adulthood, I had remembered and secretly hoped someone had destroyed that card, for such aspirations had long since faded. How noble to envision going halfway round the world to do the Lord's work! But here, in my own hometown with no praise, no accolades. What a difference!

I was finally able to laugh with God at myself. God does answer prayer, our sincere desire. He may be slow, but he never forgets the intent of our hearts. Also, he provides mirrors to show us up for what we really are. I had to confess my love for praise and approval. I had to ask myself, "Are all my motives prompted through self-seeking? Do I really care about people and human relations?" These questions called for honesty and inner searching. Thank God, that he, who reminds us of our failures and our secret, selfish desires, also forgives.

How does one get his words and his life together? How can the mind and the emotions track like hinds' feet? Is the constant cry of youth—"Hypocrites, all you church-going people"—justified? As I have had to face up to my own inconsistencies, I can't help wondering whether our fragmented society is not just a gigantic display of our inner falseness.

Daily for six years, I viewed the gaps in today's world in microcosm. Although my work in human relations dealt primarily with black-white relationships, my office brought before my gaze all the tensions within the community. There I saw separation afflicting many groups. So wide was it that I began to think in terms of one group's watching with distrust and suspicion its antagonist across a huge abyss. One side feels threatened by the other, and attitudinal positions are taken. Persons of divergent views often appear like angry adolescents who draw a line and dare their opponents to step over it.

How hard it is to avoid this. After struggling to be freed from some of my inbred racial prejudices, I found myself becoming "prejudiced against those still prejudiced." What a senseless battle. Does one defend one's position, attempting to convert? To talk out of both sides of the mouth may be politic, but it is impossible for me.

I remember being faced with this dilemma one day when I was to speak to the Rotary Club. Since my husband had been a Rotarian and I knew most of the members, I would have liked to make an innocuous talk with which none could disagree. However, I was painfully aware of the recent hurt inflicted on a black friend by his having been denied club membership. At the same time, I was fully conscious of the many worthy projects of the club, chief among them the student loan program which benefits black as well as white.

How must I speak, knowing there was within that group of men the economic and political power to make any change needed in the community if there were the will? How could I speak other than from the standpoint of our need to be cognizant of the basis for black-white tensions, our refusal to be one family under God as he planned from the beginning?

I discovered I could not be true to anything I believed and follow the suggestion of not mixing religion and human relations. Regardless of being misunderstood by whites who thought I was in city hall to stir up trouble, or by blacks who thought I was not moving fast enough, I found I could answer to only one voice, the voice of God.

God even required that I witness to this decision in front of the commission in city council chamber. I struggled to evade this command, but he gave me no rest. The only way I could know peace was through obedience.

My prayer partner and I had laughingly said we might

wind up handing out tracts on the street corner, but never had I thought that I would be required to witness in city hall. Quite naturally, the commission members looked at me somewhat askance as I told them that though they could fire me, I could not obey them if their requests differed from those given me by the One to whom I must listen and submit.

Once I demonstrated my willingness to obey, even at such a cost to pride, there was a great freedom. I even began to see the reason why God had placed me there. It became plain to me that even though my role might be called that of change agent, I was there, not to change people, but to listen and to love. I was able to forget the "don't mix religion and human relations in city hall" no matter who said it.

The unity that I have sought between seemingly conflicting ideas has brought me to a great awareness of, and appreciation for, the paradox. Without it, there can be no understanding of the Christian faith. Most of us spend so much time jumping from one side of an issue to the other, or defending the stand we've taken, that we never enlarge our horizons to include both. With each new situation we seem to think there is an either/or rather than a both/and.

Having cut my religious teeth on James' oft-quoted "Faith without works is dead," I thought works meant projects. The busier I was in serving God, the more points to my credit and the more pleasing I would be to him. Socially sensitive (for which I give thanks to my church), I rushed in whenever there was a need to be met, completely unaware that Jesus had never used need as his standard of behavior. His key was obedience. He was ever watching the Father and doing as he did. Once we take a stand, whether for the personal or the social gospel, we assume we have to defend our position. Often our stance becomes rigid. To refuse to change is to refuse to grow. Why do we dislike change so much when it is so inevitable? It has been said, and no doubt correctly, the seven last words of the church will be, "We never did it that way before."

As I sought a unified life rather than a separated one—personal versus social, sacred versus secular—I had to rethink my Christian faith. Wholeness requires spirit, mind, and body to work in unison. When I took the job in city hall, I knew God was telling me to get it together, to make my words become flesh. To be in the world, but not of the world was my assignment. And it was difficult. However, there could have been no more challenging schoolroom.

I soon found out you can learn from everyone and everything. There again, I had been sorting and discarding—to my loss. As I grew to expect each person, each experience, to be an opportunity for learning; I discovered I was being taught how people think, how people react or respond, how and why people protect themselves.

Deeply involved with the many social issues, I had to come to the realization that that which gets your attention gets you. If you keep your eyes on the world too long, even for the purpose of serving the world, you become worldly.

Years ago I had read a book that referred to John R. Mott, Nobel Peace Prize winner in 1946, and his work as international president of the YMCA. What caught my attention was his practice—even with increased responsibilities—of giving not one hour daily as had been his custom, but two hours, to devotional reading and prayer.

Even though I glossed over it at the time, it evidently made an impression on me for I was reminded of this when my job in human relations was more than I alone could handle. Soon I learned that I must spend much more time "on my knees."

Daily it was my duty to deal with the hurts, the agonies, the injustices, and inequities in our society. What a high price has been paid to separate people, what damages have resulted. It was difficult for me not to let my righteous indignation become destructive human anger. The peace I had found to be real in the secret place of the Most High God must become just as real in the midst of tension-filled meetings where emotions run high.

No organization, no council, no agency, regardless of how excellent, regardless of how high their motives, will be able to create a climate of unity. My experience has convinced me of the truth of Paul's statement to the Ephesians. "For Christ is our living peace. He has made us both one by breaking down the barrier and enmity which lay between us" (Eph. 2:14 Phillips).

For many years, most of my associates were people of similar views and backgrounds—people who went to *my* church, who belonged to *my* club, who shared *my* interests and opinions, whether it was in a bridge club, a book club, or the League of Women Voters. My first CFO expanded my world. High church, low church; rich, poor; old, young; liberal, fundamental—all were there. The power of Christ's magnetism was manifest for he promised, "And I, when I am lifted up from the earth, will draw all men to myself" (John 12:32).

Theologically, we were poles apart; politically, all varieties; yet we were one. This oneness was again impressed upon me when members of the Kentucky CFO Council Ring were in a circle of prayer about the election which was coming up the following week. As I stood holding hands with persons whose political loyalties I knew to be opposite from mine, I marveled that we could all be praying that God's will be done.

Getting it all together does not imply rubber-stamp copies. Rather, it is an appreciation of differences, a thankfulness for the diversity within the unity. Truth is always paradoxical.

Is it possible to have strong conviction, yet recognize the paradox? Do we become so aware of the many different viewpoints that our position wavers and everything becomes relative? Does it mean analyzing every question until paralysis sets in?

A Christian must learn to distinguish between half-truth and the whole truth. This is the difficulty and the glory of the Christian faith. That God became man defies human reasoning. Therefore, we who would seek him through the intellect alone have to be consistent and whittle Jesus down to our own size. Those whose faith is based primarily on the sovereignty of God would never dare question and will never know Jesus as man.

A conversation with a friend, a Roman Catholic nun, made this very clear to me. We had to laugh when I found myself trying to "convert" her to the divinity of Christ. For many years, she had thought of Jesus only as God—she had half-truth. For many years, I had thought of Jesus only as man—I had half-truth. After being freed, we both had changed our positions and had almost swung to the opposite view rather than recognize the whole truth, Jesus is truly God, truly man.

As we seek wholeness in relationships, we have to consider the difference in roles and the uniqueness of each. What is God's role? What is mine? What does "You, therefore, must be perfect, as your heavenly Father is perfect" (Matt. 5:48), really mean? Often it is skipped over as impossible, but we err when we toss out any scripture. A helpful insight into that verse for me is that each of us is to fulfill the function for which we are made, just as God perfectly fulfills his role.

Once started on this spiritual pilgrimage, it becomes quite evident that we have usurped the role of God, or at least attempted to. Like that first Adam, we want to be god. We want to know all and have all power. We want to control our lives, and what changing is to be done we want to do. We make plans relying on our limited compassions, our limited insights. Often, sincerity of desire is confused with rightness. Yet, we need to ask, Is there right and wrong? Have we lost all sense of sin? In learning forgiveness, have we forgotten that as you sow, you will reap?

How do we get it all together? How can we have strong convictions without becoming dogmatic? How can we keep open minds without becoming shallow? Why is today's liberal threatened by the evangelical and vice versa? Why is the institutional church threatened by the charismatic and other "turned-on" movements? Have we, the church, abdicated our role and left the changes in our society to be undertaken by the humanists?

THEN COMES THE JOY

Anyone aware of today's problems has heard people say with alarm, "Why do *they* act as they do?" *They* are usually people of different races, different religious beliefs, or different social mores. If we would take the time to study our past, we could begin to see why persons act exactly as they do. Why those raised in a permissive society want to hear a voice that speaks with authority. Why those who need to get the attention of the public have to be horribly noisy. How the lowering of morals—the "anything goes" of movies, TV, books—affects the whole community.

As I view our confused world, I have to come back to my individual role. I have to confess I have tried to play god. I have sought to change people (of course, for *their* good). I have sought to change myself. God never planned it that way.

It was with great expectations that the Commission on Human Relations instigated the youth-police dialogues in city council chamber. My office had been receiving numerous complaints from youth about police harassment, and it was felt that a series of "rap" sessions would give youth and police opportunity to talk out their differences and, as a consequence, come to understand and accept one another. Monthly, these meetings were conducted under the able leadership of Dr. Robert B. Sivley, director of the Pennyroyal Regional Mental Health Center and chairman of the commission. Each group had time for dialogue in a nonthreatening atmosphere. It did not take long for some of the angry youth to verbalize their opinion of "pigs" and for some of the police to admit that any youth with long hair was immediately suspected of being a drug pusher.

108

GETTING IT ALL TOGETHER

These dialogues drew large crowds, but when they ended I seriously questioned whether any minds had been changed or prejudicial attitudes altered. Only as there is a *willingness* to be changed can lives be made different. God gives us the right of choice. If we want a changed society, there must be radically changed people. Techniques and education have failed. Only God can make new men.

As I have studied the problems of human relations, I have come to the conclusion that I cannot take sides. A larger view is necessary. Likewise, I cannot choose between the active and the passive life—I must have both. I cannot decide between being teacher and learner—I must be both. I cannot even decide between speaking and listening—I must do both.

I have seen great compassion demonstrated among humanists. I have seen lack of concern exhibited among some who wear the badge of Christian. Should Christians be different? Really a peculiar people of whom Peter speaks? Where does humanism break down? These are some of the questions that have puzzled me. Is wholeness possible in a broken world?

Can the intellectual and the spiritual meet? Can insights of psychology be of value without giving them the allegiance owed God alone? Shall we continue to do all the planning to save the world, or shall we dump it all into the lap of God? How does one who really cares, who hears the cry for help, respond? For one whose heart has been broken and who yearns to be a part of the healing process, what is the answer?

"It all makes sense!" I heard myself say aloud with almost a shout of triumph. In my search, I had unearthed a jewel. Many others have already found it, but the discovery had to be my own. I could not find it vicariously. The gem shown with a wondrous light. Like the blind man, I said, "Now I see!"

It seems so simple, there is a hesitancy to speak of it. Yet to me, it meant the end of much of my questioning. The treasure long-hidden was: *Christ must be the center of all endeavors.*

If I place human relations at the center and Christ on the periphery, this is humanism that ultimately fails. If I put Christ at the center, then everything falls into its appropriate place. His plan assures victory. And, I had rather fail in that which will ultimately succeed than succeed in that which will ultimately fail.

God sent his Son into the world to save us, and how we need saving. We don't need a Band-Aid to cover the sore, we need radical surgery to root out the disease. Reformation requires transformation.

I sought to be open and became shallow. I sought the universal and lost the personal. I sought the relative and lost the absolute. I sought relevance and wandered aimlessly in the peripheral.

I sought Jesus and found wholeness. He truly is the all in all, the Word made flesh, God—man. *In him all things hold together.*

Chapter Nine

Promptings of the Spirit

An occasional mention of the Holy Ghost was somewhat frightening to my childish mind. I cannot recall any sermons or books on the subject until a few years ago. Just why the Third Person of the Godhead has been eliminated from the teachings of our more traditional churches, I do not know. It may be due to the same fear that seized me when, in the early 1960s, I was asked, "Did you receive the Holy Spirit when you believed?"

The question threatened me. It seemed to imply that my relationship with God had little significance. So, I rebelled and withdrew. Why does the new pose such a problem?

The question did drive me to the Bible, and I soon discovered that there is biblical basis for asking. Although I had grown up thinking that certain gifts, certain experiences, were the exclusive right of first-century Christians, God had refuted that for me through firsthand healings.

As I searched the Scriptures, I concluded that certain chapters of the Bible either had to be tossed out or they had to be accepted. They could no longer be ignored. As I studied that rugged band of early believers who turned the world upside down, I had to admit that by comparison, today's church looked weak and impotent. This led me to seek the secret for the change that came over those disciples in the time between the crucifixion of Jesus and the beginning of their ministry. What, really, were they like before Pentecost?

Despite their close walk with Jesus, despite their training under the Master, they lacked the power that he had. He had told them, "Truly, truly, I say to you, he who believes in me will also do the works that I do; and greater works than these will he do, because I go to the Father" (John 14:12). Was not his expectation of them exaggerated?

He was their perfect example. He gave them a set of attitudes "to be," but they knew—as anyone knows who has tried—they could never measure up. They could never do that which was expected. The key to the mystery had to be revealed and experienced.

They knew him to be victor even over the grave. The Resurrection proved that the last enemy, death, was defeated. What looked like tragic failure was transformed into the greatest triumph the world has ever known. Every claim that Jesus made was validated. He truly was the Son of God. Their long-awaited Messiah had been sent by God to save the world.

Then followed forty glorious days when he appeared to them in his resurrected body, demonstrating that God is able to do amazing things—totally unlike, and surpassing, human endeavors. During this time, he let them know that in a new way, he would be with them always. Before his ascension, he gave them final instructions: "Wait until you are empowered from on high. Wait until the same Spirit that moved across the world in the beginning, the same Spirit that overshadowed Mary bringing forth the God-man, comes to you. Wait and pray. Do not rush out with your own limited power. Wait until you are sufficiently equipped." And they waited. They had learned the importance of obedience.

With the rush of a mighty wind Pentecost came, and the church was born. God's power through the Holy Spirit was shed abroad and many signs accompanied him. Those disciples who had been fearful became courageous. Those who had been timid had holy boldness. Those who had been impotent were so filled with the Spirit that they could do the very same things that Jesus did. Now, they were equipped with the gifts that were needed to make their ministry dynamic. The Spirit moved, and the course of history was changed.

Thank God we live in a day when we are seeing the Holy Spirit pouring out his power as the prophet Joel predicted. In many ways, we are reminded that he is present and actively at work. Even though we often stand confused and ignorant of his manifestations, we need to be on guard not to quench the Spirit.

In order to be fully informed, I read not only the Bible, but writings by leaders in the charismatic movement. I had to open my mind to totally new concepts and new experiences. I had to admit that I saw a power beyond the human at work in some lives. An inheritance was mine to claim, and I had refused. I was stabbed awake, and there came a desire that would not let me rest until I had received. What a thrill to envision the church universal set aflame with the Spirit of the living God, equipped to go out in service to all mankind, enabled to change the world as that sturdy band of Christians had done about two thousand years ago. One's whole spirit is kindled at such a promise and such a prospect.

Three questions had become paramount in my search. What is the ministry of the Holy Spirit? How does one receive the Holy Spirit? What difference does the Holy Spirit make in a life?

What is the ministry of the Holy Spirit? Certainly not to make a show, to make people feel good or "high." His purposes are First, to glorify Jesus. If the name of Jesus is not magnified, be on your guard. Second, to equip the saints (Christians). Every follower of Jesus needs divine equipment. Third, to interpret the Word. How thrilling it is to have the Word illuminated where before there had been lack of understanding. Jesus promised, "The Counselor, the Holy Spirit, whom the Father will send in my name, he will teach you all things, and bring to your remembrance all that I have said to you" (John 14:26). Fourth, to intercede. We are promised that when we do not know how to pray as we ought, the Spirit will intercede for us.

How does one receive the Holy Spirit? From my own experience, there must be: (1) a recognition of need, (2) a desire, (3) an asking, and (4) an openness to receive. Truly, God will hear the requests of his people. As we humble ourselves before him, as we seek his face, he will give us the Holy Spirit. "If you then, who are evil, know how to give good gifts to your children, how much more will the heavenly Father give the Holy Spirit to those who ask him!" (Luke 11:13). This scripture was the turning point in the ministry of Oswald Chambers whose book, *My Utmost for His Highest,* has been good, solid food on which I, along with thousands, have fed for a number of years.

What difference does the Holy Spirit make in a life? I have read of those who witnessed to a new power. I have observed changes in other persons' lives. However, I must witness to the many differences in my own life. There has come (1) a new freedom to be flexible, to be vulnerable, to risk failure and rejection, to love; (2) a new love of the Bible with the Holy Spirit as interpreter; (3) a new dimension to my prayer life as I learn to hallow his name and to worship through the sacraments; (4) a new spirit in my heart—a new thankfulness, a sense of gratitude, new eyes to see adventure, even in adversity; (5) a new ministry with greater wisdom and the gift of discernment.

It is exciting that many of the more traditional churches are becoming open to the movement of the Spirit. We owe a debt to those in the charismatic movement who have brought this ministry before us with such impact that we cannot ignore it. Even though I may not agree with the degree of emphasis by some on glossolalia, I thank God for those who made me search the Bible, who caused me to hunger for more of God, who forced me to see the power that is available to those who believe, and who made me claim that which is rightfully mine.

Today, I see the world "on tiptoe to see the wonderful sight of the sons of God coming into their own" (Rom. 8:19 Phillips). May we open our hearts to the ministry of the Holy Spirit and be willing to confess that under our own power, we can do nothing.

Perhaps such a pilgrimage as mine is not necessary for all, but it was required of me. For years, my faith was based on legalism, the "dos" and "don'ts" of the Old Covenant. I am aware that many Christians are still living under this same bondage. The question must be asked, What new thing was done through the life and death of Jesus?

I can remember a period prior to Easter when I prayed for God to teach me about the Crucifixion. What did the Atonement really mean? How could the blood of One, even so great a One as Jesus, save me? I had hoped that God would present me with a simple treatise on the subject. Instead, he had to break my heart in order for me to experience some of his agony. We must experience in lesser degree the pain which he endured. My pride had to be ground in a crucible before the eyes of my heart were enlightened. God is not willing for us to have mere intellectual information. He wants us to possess and participate in the Spirit he gives.

As I began to see the deeper meaning in, and the need for, the Crucifixion, I could enter the thrill of the Resurrection. Even then, the ascended Christ had little meaning. However, Paul's letters to the Romans and to the Ephesians gave me glimpses of the truth of our position with Christ. Christ wants to be more than an example, more than a savior, more, even, than Lord. He, through the Spirit, wants to be enabler, empowerer, equipper.

As I saw new truth, I understood the meaning of his story of the vine and the branch. I saw how the branch provided life for the vine which bore the fruit. How gracious of God. He not only will be *with* us. He will abide *in* us, work *through* us, and appear *as* us. But the glory belongs to him. The life comes from him. The work is his.

Many times I have attempted to bear fruit without even being attached to the vine. May we, like the early church, learn to wait, to pray, and to receive the Holy Spirit, the divine Enabler. For, Pentecost *is* repeatable.

> Come, Holy Spirit come . . .
> > come as the wind and cleanse;
> > come as the fire and burn;
> > come as the light and reveal.
> Convict, convert, consecrate us, Lord,
> > until we are wholly thine. Amen.

Chapter Ten

Trust Walk

The porch swing was a special place at my childhood home. It was my mother's favorite spot for spending the late summer afternoon. People often told me they really came to expect to see her there visiting with Daddy or neighbors who had dropped by for a chat. I was sitting in this same old-fashioned swing the morning after her unexpected death, listening with half an ear to remarks made by friends who had gathered. Suddenly, I became aware that I knew exactly what my mother's response would have been to the conversation. So attuned to her thinking was I that her thoughts were known to me. As I considered this closeness, deep within me came the still, small voice saying, "When you have listened to Me as long as to your mother, when you have lived with Me as long as you have with your mother, you will know My thoughts. You will know my every response."

What an amazing union, even more remarkable than the like-mindedness between two persons. When such a relationship between God and ourselves is established, we no longer have to take our spiritual temperature. We no longer have to ask if God hears and answers prayers. We no longer wonder about God's will. We are God's will.

When I first heard Norman Grubb say, "You are God's will," I immediately thought, heresy. My unwillingness to readily accept a new concept caused Norman to call me his "greatest theological wrestler." His statement is startling, but besides shock value, it contains a deep, hidden truth. Few might be so daring, but "you are God's will" sounds much like a statement of Jesus or Paul.

Sometimes we forget our goal as Christians: to know Him, not just intellectually, but through a relationship so close that only that of Father-child adequately describes it; to live in union with him until there is no separation; to manifest his victory in every daily experience.

Most of us stop too soon. We remain babes in Christ and never develop into mature persons spiritually. Complacency sets in and we are apt to become satisfied with the mediocre. We need to feed on his Word until it is assimilated into our very beings. We take digested books about the Bible rather than the strong diet of God's Word. "But I don't get a thing from reading the Bible," many have said to me. I know, for all of us start with diluted forms. But I have learned to depend on the promise made in James, "If any of you lack wisdom, ask God who gives to all men generously" (1:5).

When my grandson, not quite four, asked, "Mommy, where does Jesus live?" her answer was, "Allen, he lives in heaven, and he will live in your heart if you let him." For a four-year-old this mystery was not difficult to accept. After thinking for a moment, he said, "Jesus lives in my heart and I live in his."

Can you blame Jesus for having such a fondness for children? They dare to believe the impossible—nothing is "too good to be true." Adults have made a god of common sense. Often our reasonable, rational approach hinders our ability to envision, and action is stymied. I recall a dream and a daring.

Our couples interdenominational prayer group had dreamed of a Kentucky Camp Farthest Out. In the spring of 1960, Louise Eggleston was in our town, and we shared our hope with her. A week later in Louisville, she announced publicly that there was to be a Kentucky CFO in the fall. That was the nudge we needed. Three of us went down to Kenlake Hotel on Kentucky Lake and rented the entire hotel for one week, not knowing whether there would be any others beside our own small group. But God honored our daring by sending over seventy people that first year. As I remember that, it still amazes me. Yet each day should be lived in absolute trust that God will bring to fruition any dream he plants within our hearts.

God wants us to step out into the deeps of life, secure in the knowledge that he is in control. He knows that spontaneity and willingness to try new experiences, to welcome new adventures, can never be ours until we are set free from the rigidity of adulthood.

An exercise designed to overcome this inflexibility, is called a trust walk. A group is divided into couples and each person takes a turn being blindfolded and led around by a partner. It is somewhat frightening at first, and many show strong resistance. So accustomed are we to the gift of sight, so eager are we to control situations, we become uptight and unyielding when we find ourselves at the mercy of someone else. Yet, I remember Lydia Lee, a young girl from Mississippi relating her feelings after this exercise, "Why, I would have gone *anywhere* with Sarah."

Our spiritual journey is a trust walk, one entered somewhat fearfully. With the first evidence of the reality of God, we take a timid step forward. Our confidence increases with knowledge of his trustworthiness, and yielding ourselves to him becomes easier as our assurance grows. To question his faithfulness indicates how little we really know God.

When our trust walk starts we are like beginners at swimming who need the security of being able to touch the bottom of the pool. I can see the tense bodies of adults when my daughter is teaching them to swim. How much harder for an adult to learn than a child. Whereas children delight in water splashed, adults withdraw and try in vain to keep their faces dry. Only as we give ourselves to the water do we learn that it will support us. Then comes the joy. The tragedy is that some never discover the joy of the Lord—they never let go and let God be God.

As trust in the Father develops, a new dimension is entered. We begin to think his thoughts, to glimpse new truth, to be sensitive to the promptings of the Spirit, and to sense the meaning of holiness. As I look back, I can see God's hand so clearly directing my path even before I knew him. How thrilling to get an inkling of his design, to discover the truth of his promises, and to claim them as ours for they are available to everyone.

How simple it sounds—simple, yet hard. We have been programmed to become self-sufficient, self-confident. Proverbs have been quoted until we believe we are to "stand on our own two feet" without any consideration of others. "Master of our fate" has been drilled into our subconscious until nothing short of total helplessness prepares us for the role of yielding, trusting.

Fear grabs us like a dark monster. We are afraid to trust persons or God. Our training has made us believe that we are to be "strong." To admit weakness is devastating to pride and without pride, we crumble. Our own status is sometimes determined by others, by who is above us or below. I recall a sociology class in our community college to which I spoke on the subject of human relations and prejudice. After a presentation, I sought to get the class involved in discussion. It became obvious that two young students were extremely prejudiced, all the while claiming not to be. Finally, some word ignited and the spokesman angrily declared, "The trouble with the world is that the 'niggers' don't have anybody to look down on."

How sad to build one's ego by feeling superior to others. Prejudice is not limited to race, and most of us have to deal with it.

My years in city hall made me look at the reasons we use to protect ourselves. Hurts cause us to run for cover; pride requires pretense (a mask we dare not remove). We distrust persons we do not know. All these things make us hide behind walls of our own making. Sometimes those walls become high and firm before we see they have enclosed us, and we are prisoners.

A perfect example of trust is in the story of Peter when Jesus called him to step out of his boat and walk. Jesus invites us to do the impossible also. He calls us to forget the common sense and to step out without a thought of how ridiculous we look trying to "walk on water." How significant are the recorded words, for it was only when Peter took his eyes off Jesus and looked down that he became frightened and began to sink. Jesus calls each of us to step out of whatever earthly safety and security we have.

After being placed in city hall in the job of director of Human Relations, I was called out. Doubts began to come. Was I hearing Him aright? Was it wishful thinking? What about my motives? These had to be examined, and I discovered that it was not escapism. Having overcome a number of the inner and outer conflicts connected with the job, I was quite comfortable there and would have been glad to stay on a few years longer.

To what was God calling me? This was the real problem. He gave me no answer, yet he gave me no rest. His only reply to my questioning seemed to be, "Just be available to me."

I found eating words very distasteful. I had questioned persons' "being called of God" not too many years before. So I was not surprised at the reaction of the mayor and the commission when I told them of God's call and my decision to resign. They were truly concerned for me and seemed alarmed when I told them I had no job to which I was going. Other than some speaking engagements, I had no plans. They urged me to reconsider, and I was grateful for their evidenced caring. They tried to hide their fear for my future (and maybe even my sanity). It was a rather sad parting, for each person with whom I worked I had grown to love.

Since stepping out of "my boat," I've been given repeated assurances of the rightness of my hearing. God has opened many doors. My faith in his ability has grown.

Awareness of my need for the "single eye" has sharpened. To listen and to look to Jesus *only* has become imperative.

Why tell my story? Again, it is in response to His request. Perhaps my friend Althea confirmed it in a way that even she does not know. Some years before I told her of the sinking feeling I had when I was to speak to a large prayer group in Atlanta. When the minutes were read, I heard that their speaker the preceding month had been Corrie Ten Boom. After such a person, who was I? What did I have to share of comparable worth? Althea's response was, "After all, not many of us have ever been in a concentration camp. But every person can identify with an ordinary person like you." So, Althea and Mary Webster are both right. God is desperate. He will use anybody who trusts him and will obey him. His only requirement is our availability. It is his ability. To him be the glory!

How he wants to turn our fears to faith, our tragedies to triumph, our sorrows to joy. As we allow him to give us a new Spirit, we can echo the words of C. S. Lewis, "In Christianity God is not a static *thing*—not even a person—but a dynamic, pulsating activity, a life, almost a kind of drama. Almost, if you won't think me irreverent, a kind of dance. The union between the Father and the Son is such a live concrete thing that this union itself is also a Person."

Chapter Eleven

No Stopping Place

"Together, let us make this a city under God" were the words printed on a giant poster I had in the office of Human Relations where I served for six years. On the poster were two hands of different colors clasped in a compact of friendship.

Daily I prayed that this become a reality, not only for our city, but for our nation. As I prayed, God gave me a glimpse of a city under God where love prevailed, where fear of differences no longer threatened, where each person grew to appreciate diversity. A city where God was reverenced as the Almighty to whom we all bowed.

God has placed a tremendous yearning in my heart that we be daring enough and trusting enough to follow him who said, "I am the Way," to live in accordance with his plan, to allow him to love through us. Just for one moment dream with me of a city where each man looks at every other and sees the potential for good, where trust replaces distrust and faith replaces fear.

THEN COMES THE JOY

A foolish dream? I don't believe so. Else, why would Jesus have invited us to live in his kingdom here and now?

It is never too late to start. Yet, we never arrive. Each glimpse of truth reveals that there is so much more, each step which brings us closer to God makes us aware of his magnitude. The "much mores" of God tease us to come out into the wideness of his grace, to learn how deep and wide and great is the love of Christ.

God gave me a special blessing by allowing me to spend one whole day with Dr. Frank Laubach just a few weeks prior to his unexpected death. There were no questions to ask him, no deep mysteries to explore, only a love to share. I wanted to thank him and to tell him that my soul's sincere desire was to create in others the hunger to know God that he, twenty years before, had created within me. As we spoke of prayer and his life of prayer, I shall never forget his words, "Mary Virginia, I feel as if I've just begun."

Frank Laubach is considered by many to be more like Brother Lawrence than any man of our century. If at eighty-seven he could say he felt as if he'd just begun, why should I be impatient? Why expect instant maturity? Why struggle to arrive?

Estelle Carver was in my home shortly after her eightieth birthday. She was full of dreams for the future. Sharing with me a thrilling new avenue of service opening for her, she said, "After all, Moses just started out when he was eighty." How grateful I am for teachers who demonstrated that it is magnificent to grow old if you keep young.

A darling young girl named Julie came to an Adventure in Prayer I was leading in Mayfield, Kentucky. She was wearing a button different from the many I had seen. "I am a C.U.C." When asked the meaning, she gaily replied, "I am a Christian under construction." And so are we all.

Even Paul, the greatest missionary the world has ever known, said at the close of his life that his goal was "to know Christ." After years of preaching, John Wesley saw a light and rushed into a room where a group had gathered for prayer and shouted, "I believe." Frank Laubach at eighty-seven could say, "I have just begun."

We are chosen to live in a day when man's plans and efforts end in disillusionment; when all the wonders of technology still do not answer the ultimate questions of life; when even the best of minds and the best of philosophies leave youth purposeless and despairing. Could it be that we have planned without God? God who made us is abundantly able to reveal and execute his divine plan for the earth he created. Jesus perfectly modeled a life-style which he told us all to live. He invited us to share in his kingdom and promised us his Spirit, which is absolutely essential for kingdom-living. So faithful is he that we can say with Paul, "I do concentrate on this: I forget all that lies behind me and with hands outstretched to whatever lies ahead I go straight for the goal—my reward the honour of my high calling by God in Christ Jesus" (Phil. 3:13, 14 Phillips).

We can thank God that we have been brought to a point in history when a radical change is demanded. How great is our hope when, in a day such as ours, we, the recipients of God's grace, can claim the promise, "Where sin increases, grace abounds much more."

When I knew the Lord to be calling me out of the security of job and place, I shared with my friend Reg Goff, founder of Prayer Unlimited. Reg asked me on what foundation I was basing my call. Unhesitatingly, the answer came, "On the promise of Jesus that if I seek his kingdom first, he will provide all things." Reg was satisfied that I stood on solid ground.

Vulnerable though we be, he will not leave us unprotected. Inside the circle of his love, we *can* live in the kingdom of God, a kingdom unseen by men, but very real, very practical, and eternal.

How wonderfully God has honored my obedience. He has let me begin to enter his rest. He has expanded my world and my ministry in such amazing ways that each day begins with great expectation and anticipation. How can I but thank him and pray that each person comes to know him who has turned my mourning into dancing?

We are told by Meister Eckhart, "There is no stopping place in this life—no, nor was there ever one for any man, no matter how far along his way he'd gone. This above all, then, be ready at all times for the gifts of God and always for new ones."